EASY AND INVENTIVE VEGETARIAN SUPPERS

Vegetables

MARK DIACONO

Hardie Grant

QUADRILLE

For my daughter Nell, who makes me happier than anyone has a right to be.

INTRODUCTION

It is a miracle that we find ourselves on (as far as we know) the only planet with life. For this, we owe the few centimetres of topsoil that covers much of it. That a great diversity of plants that spring from this life-giving layer are edible – providing us with energy and nutrients in small, combined quantities that are perfectly suited to our thriving – is almost beyond belief. That many are delicious – or can be made so thanks to centuries of experimentation – is astonishing.

And yet here we are.

Humans could live a healthy life consuming almost only the group of edible plants we call vegetables, yet somehow the complications of modern life and the interests of certain multinational shareholders have encouraged us to a place where many are over-fed and under-nourished.

A great deal of the remedy to this lies within Michael Pollan's 7-word food manifesto: Eat food, mostly plants, not too much.

The simplest, most pleasure-giving route to that uncomplicated holy land is to open our minds and kitchens to the joys of eating the best of what's in season.

Many of us would like to put vegetables at the centre of what we eat, to consume more of them and perhaps fewer highly processed foods; to create simple, nourishing meals using vegetables all year round. That is what this book is for.

It is full of simple, seasonal, home-cooked main meals with vegetables very much at their heart, making the most of readily available fresh produce whether homegrown or bought.

I hope you will find it utterly useful: it is the answer if you are, like me, one of those who wants to maximize the amount and diversity of vegetables in their diet, who wants a great range of seasonal meat-free suppers to turn to on a wet Wednesday evening in December or a lazy summer Sunday.

If eating healthily is your priority, the recipes in these pages will not only nourish you, they will help encourage your internal microbiome to thrive. Our gut is populated by numerous types of beneficial bacteria that work to our physical and mental benefit; this microbiome thrives on a diverse diet of plants. Eating vegetables rich in fibre, polyphenols and other health-promoting compounds is the huge step towards a healthy future. If that sounds good to you, the only question to answer is 'how can I make doing that delicious?'

As I'll show you, it's easy and simple to get plenty of flavourful, seasonal vegetables into your diet, without thinking too hard about it. With almost everything, I find one simple commitment more effective than innumerable daily decisions where you are counting how many of this or that you are eating. Pick a number between 1 and 7 – the number of evenings you can reliably commit to eating with vegetables to the fore – and you'll be living a healthier life, filled with food you were made to eat.

These pages include close to 100 recipes, almost all main courses (in truth, it's more like 300 recipes, as each is highly adaptable to what's in season, with easy substitutions included throughout). And most of them can be bent into lunch or even breakfast in some cases.

I wanted these recipes to be almost entirely dinner-friendly. I have so many excellent vegetarian books that are filled predominantly with side dishes and, love them as I do, they aren't the answer to what I want when a long day at work is met by the longest of dark evenings.

This book is for everyone. The recipes are completely vegetarian without compromising on delicious flavour. You'll not find even an anchovy. If you eat a plant-based diet, all but a couple of recipes offer options whereby eggs and dairy can be omitted or substituted. Many people have an intolerance of gluten; I've offered alternatives.

Hey omnivores. This book is also for you. I'm going to save myself a thousand words by not adding 'this is incredible with roast lamb' or 'serve with roast chicken'. You know how good vegetables are as a side; I'm hoping that by the time you've made some of these recipes, you'll see how exceptional they are as the main event.

My desire is that this book will encourage you to strengthen your relationship with the seasons. Eating is at its most rewarding when it is tied to the time of year. The best winter produce where you live is so superior to summer ingredients flown in from somewhere else. More than that, once you connect to the food that appears throughout the year, the end of its peak becomes part of its pleasure, ushering in, as it always does, another delicious vegetable in its place.

Surrender to the gloriousness of local asparagus' short spring season, and you'll be ruined for the bland green pencils from Peru that act as a ropey tribute-band for the rest of the year. More than that, the crossover of the last asparagus with the earliest peas is a coming-together all the more sweet for its brevity. The joyous following on from one vegetable to the next means kitchen life just changes rather than dips. It's the same when Jerusalem artichokes arrive just as homegrown tomatoes finally give up the ghost. And on it goes. This, my friend, is perhaps the greatest pleasure of putting real food at the centre of your life: there is always something equally delicious to look forward to.

It is surprisingly simple to achieve; the smallest of behavioural shifts, repeated. While supermarkets will always offer pleasureless tomatoes in the middle of winter, they sit alongside what is beautifully in season where you live, and when that's a celeriac soon to become a creamy dauphinoise, seasonality tastes mighty fine. It's just a matter of reaching for one rather than the other – of choosing a healthier life filled with deliciousness – and this book will help you do that with confidence.

Eating seasonal vegetables grown in your own country will engage you with the best of the seasons and the benefits that come with it. If you can shorten that chain still further to buy from greengrocers, farmers' markets, direct from the producer or via a veg box scheme – perhaps even from a grower whose name you get to know – so much the better. The money you spend stays incrementally local to your location; the employment benefits very possibly affect someone you know; the landscape and biodiversity implications are ones you might well enjoy in your view. All this from eating incredible suppers with seasonal vegetables at their heart.

You'd be surprised if I didn't try to persuade you to take one more (seemingly small) step with potentially huge implications…

If you don't already, I hope you might consider growing a little of what you eat. Even a few pots of woody herbs by the kitchen door can change every meal. I know no better shortcut to engaging with where your food comes from than this. When you become a grower, no matter how small your patch, who provides sustenance for yourself and your loved ones, it's easier to empathize with the efforts of others who bring food to the rest of us. The more of us who are engaged, the better chance we have of creating a more sustainable food system for the generations that follow.

That said, if time, space or inclination dissuade you from anything more than eating more vegetables, that's the greatest step right there. If all you do is shop as normal but with seasonality in mind, then your life and diet will be enriched.

Whatever else we may choose to eat, vegetables are essential to a life-giving, nutritious diet. This book helps you do that in the best way of all: in plentiful, delicious mouthfuls.

Veg wi

th eggs

HUEVOS ROTOS

If you just happen to have 'accidentally' boiled 800g too many new potatoes as I seem to rather too often, this is where they should find a home. Likewise, the first small spinach leaves of the year. That said, this is perfectly good later in the year, even if the spinach is larger, as long as the potatoes are on the waxy side. This makes a great easy supper, quickish lunch or – as I most often have it – weekend breakfast. If it pleases you to add bacon, halloumi or a few cubes of fried tofu, don't be shy.

Serves 2–4

50ml (2fl oz) olive oil

2 garlic cloves, finely chopped

400g (14oz) can chopped tomatoes

2–3 tsp guajillo chilli flakes, or your favourite chillies

800g (1lb 12oz) boiled new potatoes, cut into bite-sized pieces

50g (2oz) baby spinach

4 eggs

sea salt and freshly ground black pepper

Heat half the olive oil in a medium frying pan over a medium heat, add the garlic and fry for a minute to soften. Add the tomatoes, half the chilli flakes and a big pinch of salt and simmer for about 15 minutes until thick and rich.

Meanwhile, fry the potatoes in the remaining oil in a large frying pan for 10–15 minutes until golden and beginning to crisp. Season with salt and pepper.

Stir the spinach through the potatoes until they wilt, then transfer to a plate. Add the tomato sauce to the large frying pan, spooning the potato mix on top. Use a spoon to create four hollows in the mix and break an egg into each one. Sprinkle the remaining chilli flakes over and cover with a lid. Cook over a medium heat for 7–12 minutes, depending on how you like your eggs.

VEGAN: Omit the eggs.
GF: Yes.
SEASONAL SWAPS: Use sweet potato or celeriac instead of potatoes and replace the spinach with chard, kale, beetroot (beet) or radish leaves.

TURKISH EGGS

Aka *menemen*, another of these whatever-time-of-day delights I love so much. This is totally shortcutable with canned tomatoes by the way, and do use coriander (cilantro) if you have no parsley, harissa paste instead of Turkish pepper, feta rather than halloumi, or bread rather than pitta.

Serves 4

4 tbsp extra virgin olive oil

2 onions, finely chopped

2 red (bell) peppers, finely chopped

3 garlic cloves, finely chopped

2 tbsp Turkish pepper paste, (or use 2 tbsp tomato purée/paste and 1 tsp paprika)

6 large tomatoes, peeled and finely chopped

1 tsp chilli flakes (as strong or mild as you like), plus extra to serve

4 pitta breads, chopped or torn

200g (7oz) halloumi, finely diced

small bunch of flat-leaf parsley, finely chopped

4 eggs

flaky sea salt and freshly ground black pepper

Heat half the olive oil in a large frying pan over a medium heat and cook the onions and red peppers for 10 minutes, stirring often, until softened.

Add the garlic and pepper paste and cook for 30 seconds. Add the tomatoes and cook for 5–10 minutes, stirring now and again, and using a wooden spoon to encourage them to break down and become thick. Season with salt, pepper and the chilli flakes.

Meanwhile, fry the pitta and halloumi in the remaining olive oil for 2–3 minutes until golden, then stir in half the parsley and cover to keep warm.

Break the eggs into a bowl and beat lightly, then pour into the pan with the tomato and pepper. Lower the heat and stir as you would if making scrambled eggs. With the egg only just cooked (they will continue to cook), remove from the heat, and stir in the rest of the parsley.

Serve with the halloumi and pitta scattered over, with another pinch of chilli flakes.

VEGAN: Try a handful of cooked chickpeas instead of the halloumi.
GF: Use GF pittas or bread.
SEASONAL SWAPS: There's not much to swap out for seasonality here, though I'd be tempted to use good canned tomatoes instead of fresh bland winter ones.

BUBBLE + SQUEAK

If you wake up mildly regretful, anxious and in need of stabilizing after a night where your eyes were bigger than your liver; if you reach midday and the myth of porridge keeping you sustained has made itself apparent for the nth time; if a van drove through a puddle, soaking you and your new coat as you waited at the bus stop – this is for you. The work of minutes if you have leftovers, and not much longer from scratch. A proper friend in need. A side of baked beans, broccoli, or just as it is, will bring pleasure.

Serves 4

800g (1lb 12oz) potatoes, peeled and diced

50g (2oz) butter

2 bunches of spring onions (scallions), trimmed and cut into 3cm (1¼in) lengths

100g (3½oz) kale or chard, finely chopped

3 tbsp extra virgin olive oil

300g (10oz) mushrooms, thinly sliced or pulled into thin strips

4 eggs

flaky sea salt and freshly ground black pepper

Boil the potatoes in a pan of salted water for 10–15 minutes until just tender. Drain.

Melt half the butter in a large frying pan over a medium heat and cook the spring onions until softened. Add the kale to the pan and cook for 2–3 minutes until wilted, then add the boiled potatoes and gently mash them together with the kale and onions. Allow the mixture to cook for a few minutes, stirring occasionally, until the edges become crisp and golden. Season with salt and pepper. Use a wooden spoon or similar to press the mixture to form a flat cake. Cook for a few more minutes. Using a plate, carefully flip the bubble and squeak over onto the plate, then slide back into the pan with the remaining butter and cook the other side until it's also golden and crisp.

Meanwhile, heat 2 tablespoons of the olive oil in a large frying pan over a medium-high heat. Add the mushrooms to the pan in a single layer, rather than crowd the pan (fry them in batches if needed), gently tossing now and again until they are golden. Season the mushrooms with salt and pepper, then spoon on top of the bubble and squeak.

In a separate frying pan (to avoid the eggs sticking), heat the remaining tablespoon of olive oil over a medium heat. Crack the eggs into the pan and fry to your liking.

To serve, divide the bubble and squeak and mushrooms into four and top each with an egg, seasoning with salt and pepper. I have to admit to a weakness for a dash of hot sauce here; my daughter favours ketchup; my wife looks on in disgust.

VEGAN: I think this fries to golden a little better in butter, but if that's outside your diet, use olive oil and it'll be grand.
GF: Yes.
SEASONAL SWAPS: The mushrooms are optional, but if you either have them or think ahead to get them, chanterelles or oyster mushrooms are particularly good here. The only thing that should remain constant is the proportions of carb to greenery; this can bend to whatever you have. Potatoes, sweet potato, celeriac and (in combination with potato) swede, carrots and parsnip are excellent carbs to employ, with fried onions, green beans, peas, asparagus, cabbage, sprouts and pea shoots among the very many options for the leafiness.

HUEVOS RANCHEROS

Who doesn't like the idea of a hot mid-morning Mexican treat, made to bring pleasure? Whether you are looking for weekend energy to push you into the day, reviving medicine to see you past the effects of an evening of over-refreshment, or a spicy, quick easy supper, this is for you. Serve with tortillas for authenticity, flatbreads for happiness (page 183) or excellent toast for expedience.

Serves 4

3 tbsp olive oil

1 onion, finely chopped

1 red (bell) pepper, finely chopped

1 green (bell) pepper, finely chopped

1–3 jalapeño chillies, thinly sliced

2 garlic cloves, finely chopped

1–2 tbsp chipotle paste (or use 1–2 tsp chipotle flakes, to taste)

1 tsp ground cumin

400g (14oz) can chopped tomatoes

400g (14oz) can black beans or kidney beans, drained and rinsed

4 large eggs

150g (5oz) sour cream

juice of 1 lime

small bunch of coriander (cilantro), finely chopped

flaky sea salt and freshly ground black pepper

Heat the olive oil in a large frying pan over a medium heat and cook the onion, peppers and half your jalapeños for 10 minutes until softened. Add the garlic, half your chipotle paste (or flakes) and the cumin and cook for 1 minute until fragrant.

Pour in the tomatoes and season with salt and pepper. Simmer the mixture for about 10 minutes until the sauce has thickened, then stir in the beans and heat through.

Crack the eggs into a bowl and whisk them together until well beaten.

Push the tomato and bean mixture to one side of the pan to make space for the eggs and pour them in. Allow the eggs to cook for a few seconds until they start to set around the edges. Gently scramble the eggs with a spatula, mixing them with the tomato and bean mixture. Continue stirring and cooking until the eggs are just about cooked – they will continue to cook even off the heat.

Mix your remaining chipotle into the sour cream and add the lime juice. Season with salt to taste.

Drizzle the eggs with the chipotle cream and scatter with the coriander and the rest of the sliced jalapeños.

VEGAN: Replace the eggs with a little fried tofu and use a plant-based sour cream.
GF: Yes – serve with GF tortillas, flatbreads or bread.
SEASONAL SWAPS: As this is a celebration of the Capsicum family of peppers and chillies, there are no great substitutions for those, but by all means use different beans (or indeed chickpeas) if you fancy.

KIMCHI OMELETTE

Kimchi – a garlicky, spicy, sour, salty, fermented vegetable dish, classically made with Chinese leaf – is peculiarly addictive. There is nothing subtle about it, which is exactly why it works here. You can make your own (it's surprisingly easy – find a recipe in my books *Sour* and *Ferment*, or on my website) but there are a few cracking ones widely available in the shops.

Serves 1

2 large eggs

60g (2¼oz) kimchi, drained and chopped

1 tbsp kimchi juice (liquid from the kimchi jar/packet)

1 tbsp extra virgin olive oil or butter

1 tbsp fresh chives, thinly sliced

chilli flakes, to taste

flaky sea salt and freshly ground black pepper

Crack the eggs into a bowl and beat well until fully combined. Add the kimchi and kimchi juice and mix well.

Heat the olive oil or butter in a frying pan over a medium heat, allowing it to get hot before pouring the kimchi eggs into the pan.

As the omelette begins to set at the edges, use a spatula to gently lift the edges, tilting the pan to encourage the uncooked egg to flow into the space. Sprinkle with half of the chives.

Once the omelette is mostly set but still slightly runny on top, carefully fold the omelette over, season with salt and pepper, and sprinkle with the rest of the chives and the chilli flakes.

VEGAN: I've tried to find a way that this works with egg substitutes and I've yet to succeed; apologies.

GF: Yes, but do check the label on whichever brand of kimchi you use.

SEASONAL SWAPS: If you don't have kimchi this is a pretty good template for turning whatever you have – a handful of mushrooms, some leftover potatoes, some chopped cooked greens, etc. – into a cracking breakfast or lunch.

SUMMER FRITTATA

I am very happy eating this at any hour of the day. It works as a lazy leftover breakfast, easy lunch or substantial supper, especially after a game that's run into extra time and the extra beer requires a little savoury accompaniment.

As marvellous as this is – and do make it as is, to make a friend of it – take it as a template for what each season has to offer; it even comes up trumps when you have a bowlful of leftover roast vegetables in the fridge looking for a delicious home. If you have 8 eggs, chances are your fridge will see you right for the rest in some form or other.

Serves 4

8 large eggs

80ml (3fl oz) whole milk

2 tbsp olive oil

1 red onion, thinly sliced

1 red (bell) pepper, finely chopped

1 courgette (zucchini), finely chopped

250g (9oz) cherry tomatoes, halved

small bunch fresh basil, leaves torn

50g (2oz) finely grated fresh Parmesan

flaky sea salt and freshly ground black pepper

Preheat the oven to 180°C/160°C fan/350°F.

In a large bowl, whisk together the eggs and milk with some salt and pepper until well combined.

Heat the olive oil in an ovenproof frying pan over a medium heat. Add the sliced red onion and cook for 5 minutes until it begins to soften. Add the red pepper and courgette and cook for another 4–5 minutes, stirring occasionally, until tender. Stir in the cherry tomatoes, cooking for 1–2 minutes until the tomatoes start to soften. Tip the mix out of the pan into a large bowl and add the basil. Return the pan to the stove.

Pour the egg mixture into the pan and spoon in the cooked vegetables, then sprinkle the cheese on top. Cook over a medium heat for 3–4 minutes; when the edges start to set, transfer to the oven and bake for 10–15 minutes until golden and set on top.

Remove from the oven and allow to cool for a few minutes before slicing the frittata into wedges. Serve warm or at room temperature.

VEGAN: No, but for dairy-free use a plant-based milk.
GF: Yes.
SEASONAL SWAPS: Instead of red pepper, courgette and tomato, try using boiled potatoes and fried onions, or for a spring frittata use green beans and peas or asparagus and pea shoots.

Som

nething
bready

PANZANELLA

Once upon a time, panzanella was a dish of onions and bread – and I'm sure it was delightful – but if ever a recipe summed up the best of the sunny day harvests, it's the modern tomato-heavy incarnation. Better still, this central Italian delight works beautifully for those tomatoes that have taken ripeness a little too seriously and are considering collapsing into the two-dimensional; their juiciness is perfect for the bread they accompany.

There is no cooking to transform, no magic to conjure: this is all about the excellence of the vegetables. The bread is best a day old – perhaps two or three – to add a little resistance to the juices that soak into it.

Serves 4

6 large ripe tomatoes, roughly chopped

1 red onion, thinly sliced

200g (7oz) crustless sourdough bread (a day or so old), cut into bite-sized pieces

3 tbsp red wine vinegar

90ml (6 tbsp) extra virgin olive oil

1 tbsp capers

1 small garlic clove, crushed

1 small red (bell) pepper, deseeded and thinly sliced

1 small yellow (bell) pepper, deseeded and thinly sliced

40g (1½oz) pitted black olives, like kalamata, roughly chopped

small bunch of fresh tarragon, leaves picked

flaky sea salt and freshly ground black pepper

Sprinkle the tomatoes and onion with salt and toss together. Place them in a sieve and leave the juices to drain into a bowl.

Toss the bread with the vinegar and 2 tablespoons of the oil.

Stir the capers and garlic into the drained tomato juices, then whisk in the remaining olive oil and season to taste with salt and pepper. Stir in the bread.

Combine the peppers, olives, half the tarragon and the tomato mix together in a bowl and pour over the dressed bread, tossing well.

Allow to sit for at least 20 minutes and up to 1 hour. Stir before serving scattered with the remaining tarragon.

VEGAN: Yes.
GF: Use GF bread.
SEASONAL SWAPS: Alas, it has to be summer and it has to be tomatoes.

PISSALADIÈRE

At the risk of alienating everyone I've ever met and everyone I haven't, I'm not that crazy about pizza. As much as I desire it and the first three mouthfuls please deeply, the pleasure quickly dissipates, like the second time you hear 'Mr. Blue Sky' in a summer. Give me pissaladière every time. It is – along with Zinedine Zidane and Brigitte Bardot – one of Provence's finest gifts to the world.

Traditionally made with anchovies, I've used red miso to provide the crucial savouriness, and very nicely it works too. Please don't rush the onions: once cooked, they should be barely able to pretend to hold together. And don't expect this to hang around long.

Serves 2

60ml (4 tbsp) olive oil

4 large onions, very thinly sliced

2 tsp picked fresh thyme leaves

3 tbsp red miso

about 20 pitted black olives

1 medium egg, beaten

flaky sea salt and freshly ground black pepper

For the pastry

250g (9oz) plain (all-purpose) flour, plus extra for dusting

1 tsp fine salt

125g (4½oz) chilled butter, cubed

3 tbsp iced water

Put the flour, salt and butter into a food processor and pulse until the mixture resembles fine breadcrumbs. (Alternatively, tip into a large bowl and use your fingertips to mix the butter into the flour until it resembles breadcrumbs.) Sprinkle over the water and pulse briefly until the mixture comes together (or bring together with your hands). Tip out onto a clean surface, flatten into a rough circle, wrap well, then chill for around 30 minutes.

Line a baking sheet with baking parchment. Heat the olive oil in a large pan over a low heat and very gently cook the onions with a small pinch of salt, stirring occasionally, for 30–35 minutes until they're soft and barely coloured. Season with pepper and the thyme and allow to cool.

On a lightly floured work surface, roll out the pastry to about 2mm thick and about 30cm (12in) in diameter. Slide the pastry onto the lined baking sheet and chill for 20 minutes. Meanwhile, preheat the oven to 180°C/160°C fan/350°F.

Spread the miso over the pastry, leaving a 2–3cm (1in) border around the edge. Cover the miso completely with the cooled onions, then dot with the olives. Brush the edge of the pissaladière with the egg, then bake for 40 minutes, or until the pastry is golden. Allow to cool slightly before serving, although you could also serve at room temperature.

VEGAN: Use ready-made vegan pastry and brush the edge with plant-based milk.
GF: Use GF plain flour, or try with GF ready-made pastry.
SEASONAL SWAPS: Onions are available all year round and frankly, nothing else will do.

FETA, RADISH, RHUBARB + HERBS IN PITTA

Radish's peppery bite and rhubarb's sharp edge suit each other like Jack Lemmon and Walter Matthau – a salad of both, very thinly sliced and dressed with orange juice and excellent oil, is as remarkable as it is uncomplicated – but I love this every bit as much. Everything here has its place: the feta's sour chalkiness, the sting of the onion, the zing of the herbs and lemon, anchored beautifully by the olives and the earthiness of cumin.

Easy does it with the rhubarb; you are looking to soften it only slightly in the just-boiled liquid as it cools.

Serves 4

2 tbsp white wine vinegar or cider vinegar

2 tsp sugar

3 sticks of rhubarb, thinly sliced

zest and juice of ½ lemon

300g (10oz) feta cheese, thinly sliced

1 tsp cracked cumin seeds

250g (9oz) radishes, thinly sliced

1 small red onion, very thinly sliced

1 cucumber, thinly sliced

4 pitta breads, warmed

1–2 small bunches of soft herbs (mint, tarragon, parsley, chives, dill – any mix you like), leaves only

30g (1oz) pitted black olives.

flaky sea salt and freshly ground black pepper

Bring the vinegar, sugar and 150ml (5fl oz) water to the boil, then remove from the heat. Stir in the rhubarb and allow to cool.

Grate the lemon zest over the feta and sprinkle with the cumin seeds.

Season the radishes, onion and cucumber with salt and pepper and squeeze over the lemon juice.

Slice open the pittas and fill with a little or a lot of everything, then dig in.

VEGAN: Try a plant-based feta and up the lemon a little for sourness.
GF: Use GF pittas.
SEASONAL SWAPS: Crispness, fresh crunch and the contrast with rhubarb's sourness is the key here, so swap in thinly sliced carrot, sugar snaps or mangetout for the radish, and by all means go for mango or apple slices instead of rhubarb, but tweak the lemon if needed to retain the sour edge.

ESQUITES

Lower me from a chopper to the streets of any city and I'll go in search of the best street food it offers; should I be fortunate enough for it to be a Mexican city, this is what I'd hope to find. Sweet, sour, poky and delicious.

There is a similar incarnation, elotes, where the corn stays on the cob and is either wrapped or dipped in the sauce and toppings, but if there's a chance to break out the tortillas, why not take it.

Serves 4

8 small corn tortillas (or use wheat tortillas)

2 tbsp butter

1 red onion, thinly sliced

400g (14oz) fresh corn kernels (about 4–5 ears of corn)

1 jar of roasted red or yellow (bell) peppers, torn into long strips

60g (2¼oz) mayonnaise

60g (2¼oz) sour cream

1 garlic clove, finely chopped

juice of 1 lime, plus another lime cut into wedges to serve

½–2 tsp chipotle flakes, to taste

200g (7oz) feta cheese (or Cotija cheese), crumbled

bunch of coriander (cilantro), finely chopped

sea salt and freshly ground black pepper

Preheat the oven to 180°C/160°C fan/350°F.

Place a wire rack over a baking sheet and lay out the tortillas in a single layer. Toast in the oven for 5–8 minutes until crisp. Alternatively, fry in batches in olive oil in a frying pan until crisp.

Melt the butter in a large frying pan over a low-medium heat, and sauté the onion for 7–10 minutes until soft, then add the corn kernels and peppers and cook over a high heat, stirring occasionally, for about 5–6 minutes until the corn is tender and lightly browned. Remove from the heat, allow to cool slightly and season with salt and pepper.

In a small bowl, combine the mayonnaise, sour cream, garlic, lime juice and chipotle. Stir half of this through the corn mixture.

Spread the corn and peppers on top of the tortillas. Drizzle with the remaining dressing and top with the cheese and coriander, with lime wedges on the side.

VEGAN: Use plant-based dairy alternatives.
GF: Use corn tortillas.
SEASONAL SWAPS: It has to be sweetcorn.

LEEK + SHALLOT FLAMICHE

On the day you make this Flemish marvel, try not to eat anything beforehand if you can: there is almost no chance that you will leave this alone until it has gone. When Matt (he cooks on the photoshoots) made this, he was disproportionately interested when I was taking the shot. Ordinarily too involved in cooking to eat more than the occasional mouthful, he snuck in for the first wedge the instant I'd taken the last shot. Reader, I must tell you that before the hour was out, we had seen off the entire thing. Proceed with caution.

Serves 4

½ tsp active dry yeast

400g (14oz) strong white bread flour, plus extra for dusting

2 tbsp olive oil

30g (1oz) butter

400g (14oz) leeks, trimmed and thinly sliced

1 whole egg, beaten

100g (3½oz) crème fraîche

1 tsp chopped fresh thyme leaves

¼ whole nutmeg (or to taste), grated

20g (¾oz) Parmesan or Cheddar cheese, grated

100g (3½oz) shallots, very thinly sliced

flaky sea salt and freshly ground black pepper

Mix 280ml (9½fl oz) warm water and the yeast together in a small bowl and allow to bubble for 5 minutes.

In a large bowl, stir ¼ teaspoon salt into the flour, then add the yeasty water. Pull the mix together with a large spoon to form a rough ball and tip out onto a lightly floured worktop. Knead the dough for 5 minutes until smooth and elastic, then put the dough into a clean bowl that has been greased with the olive oil. Cover with a tea towel and leave for up to 2 hours, or until almost doubled in size.

While the dough is proving, melt the butter in a pan over a medium heat and cook the leeks, stirring often, until really soft and sweet. Allow to cool. In a medium bowl, mix the egg, crème fraîche, thyme, a good pinch of salt, and an exuberance of pepper and nutmeg. Add the cooled leeks.

Preheat the oven to 230°C/210°C fan/450°F and line a 40 x 30cm (16 x 12in) baking tray with baking parchment.

Lightly flour a work surface and roll the dough out to fit the baking tray – it should be ½–1cm (¼–½in) thick. Make a small lip around the edge of the dough and spoon the leek mixture on top, spreading it out evenly. Sprinkle with the cheese and spread the shallots over the top. Place in the oven and cook for 20–25 minutes until the top is nicely coloured and the base is crisp.

Serve straight out of the oven, warm or at room temperature – it's never not good – with a tomato and or green salad.

VEGAN: Substitute the crème fraîche and cheese for plant-based and try a little whipped silken tofu in place of the egg.
GF: Try with GF ready-made puff pastry.
SEASONAL SWAPS: It really ought to be made with leeks, but onions are a pretty marvellous substitute.

Salady

things

CRISP SUMMER SALAD

Burrata and mozzarella are very closely related, though the differences are crucial. Burrata is essentially mozzarella that has been filled with a blend of soft curds and cream. It's really not very hard to fall deeply in love with it. As much as I love the fresh, contrasting flavours and textures of this salad without it (it makes a fabulous side dish like that), burrata makes a main course of it, and one of my favourite summer lunches.

This needs really good peaches or nectarines; if they are the sort that resolutely refuse to ripen, then halve, stone and roast or griddle them until just-tender and allow them to cool at least a little before using. I love whole basil leaves for this but shred them if you prefer.

Serves 4

2 ripe peaches, sliced

1 cucumber, thinly sliced

½ Chinese leaf cabbage, shredded

2 small fennel bulbs, trimmed and thinly sliced

4 tbsp extra virgin olive oil

2 tbsp red wine vinegar

2 tsp finely grated fresh ginger

1 generous ball of burrata

2 pieces of candied ginger, very thinly sliced

small bunch of fresh basil, leaves picked

1 tbsp sesame seeds, toasted

flaky sea salt and freshly ground black pepper

In a large salad bowl, combine the peaches, cucumber, Chinese leaf and fennel and season with a good pinch of salt and pepper.

In a small bowl, whisk together the olive oil, vinegar and fresh ginger to make the dressing. Season well with salt and pepper, then add to the salad and gently toss to coat all the ingredients.

Arrange the salad on a platter or individual plates, then tear the burrata into pieces and add to the top. Scatter with the candied ginger, basil leaves and sesame seeds.

VEGAN: Try fried tofu in place of the burrata; it will be very different but delicious.
GF: Yes.
SEASONAL SWAPS: Plums, apricots and exceptional apples can be used instead of the peaches, and by all means try little gems instead of the Chinese leaf.

SPRING GADO-GADO

Gado means 'mix', so the double emphasis here tells you just how much this Indonesian salad has going on. Raw and cooked vegetables, hard-boiled eggs, boiled potatoes, occasionally tofu and more – the choice is wide – but the constant is the peanut sauce. Contrast of texture is really crucial to the pleasure of this: don't overcook the vegetables and use the freshest radishes you can. The crisp onions are optional; I have a weakness for them and use the method for crisp shallots on page 68.

Serves 4

4 eggs

800g (1lb 12oz) new potatoes, peeled and cut in half

1 small spring cabbage, halved through the base leaving the stalk intact

150g (5oz) green beans, trimmed and cut into 3cm (1¼in) lengths

150g (5oz) beansprouts

10 radishes, thinly sliced

1 cucumber, thinly sliced

juice of ½ lime

crisp onions, to serve (optional)

For the peanut sauce

2 garlic cloves, roughly chopped

1 small onion, roughly chopped

½–1 tsp chilli powder

1 tsp ground cumin

1 tsp ground coriander

pinch of salt

1 tbsp vegetable oil

75g (2½oz) peanuts

200ml (7fl oz) full-fat coconut milk

2 tbsp soy sauce

juice of ½ lime

2 tbsp sugar

Put the eggs into a large pan of salted water and bring to the boil. Once the water starts boiling, cook the eggs for 6 minutes, then scoop out and cool in a bowl of cold water – keep the pan of hot water for cooking the vegetables.

Boil the potatoes for 10 minutes, then add the cabbage halves and cook for 5 minutes until the potatoes are cooked through and the cabbage is just tender. Lift out the potatoes and cabbage, saving the pan and hot water for the next step.

Add the beans to the water and cook for 2 minutes until just tender, then drain well.

To make the sauce, blend the garlic and onion with the chilli powder, cumin, coriander and salt (adding a splash of water if necessary) to a smooth paste (with a stick blender or in a small food processor). Heat the oil in a pan and fry the paste over a medium heat for 5 minutes, or until it begins to brown and stick to the bottom of the pan. Add the peanuts, coconut milk, 50ml (2fl oz) water, the soy sauce, lime juice and sugar and cook for a couple of minutes to thicken. Blend again to a smoothish sauce.

Chop the potatoes and peel and cut the eggs in half. Lay the potato and cabbage on a large serving plate, then add the green beans, beansprouts, radishes and cucumber slices and finally the eggs on top. Squeeze over the lime juice, then top with the peanut sauce, and crisp onions if using.

VEGAN: Substitute the eggs for fried tofu, a handful of fried chickpeas or roasted mushrooms.
GF: Yes.
SEASONAL SWAPS: You can really use this as a template for what's good in season – asparagus for the green beans, little gem lettuces for the cabbage – but I tend to keep the potato, radish and onion as vegetable constants.

POTATO + EGG SALAD

Who doesn't love a potato salad. And who doesn't love one with egg and cornichons – little mini-gherkins – even more. This may be the finest I've ever eaten. Lower me into a skipful of this with only a fork in one hand and I'd emerge happy, heavy and ready for more.

Watercress as an accompaniment is all but essential here, ringing the bell of the mustard's nasal punch with an even louder clang. I sometimes make this with the watercress chopped and stirred through, but increasingly I like it on the side, dressed only with a little excellent olive oil.

Serves 4

800g (1lb 12oz) new potatoes, quartered

150g (5oz) mayonnaise

2 tbsp Dijon mustard

1 shallot, finely chopped

2 celery heart stalks, finely chopped (leaves reserved and roughly chopped)

2 tbsp cider vinegar

2 hard-boiled eggs, roughly chopped

6 radishes, thinly sliced

6 cornichons or pickles, finely chopped

handful of chives, roughly chopped

a couple of chive flowers, broken into florets (optional)

bunch of watercress

a little extra virgin olive oil

flaky sea salt and freshly ground black pepper

Place the potatoes in a large pan with a generous pinch of salt and cover with cold water. Bring to the boil and cook until just tender. Drain and transfer them to a large bowl and allow to cool slightly.

In a small bowl, whisk together the mayonnaise, Dijon mustard, shallot, celery heart and cider vinegar. Season well with salt and pepper.

Pour the dressing over the warm potatoes and gently toss to coat them evenly.

Scatter the potatoes with the eggs, radishes, chopped celery leaves, cornichons and chives (and the chive flowers if using), and a generous grind of black pepper. Serve with watercress – drizzled with a little olive oil – to the side.

VEGAN: Omit the eggs and use a plant-based mayo.
GF: Yes.
SEASONAL SWAPS: The key ingredients are available all year round (use a waxy potato later in the season), other than the watercress, which can be swapped for rocket (arugula) or another lively, peppery leaf.

CAULI CAESAR SALAD

It is a peculiar thing that you can work long and hard at what you do and end up being remembered for a momentary aside. And so it is with Caesar Cardini. A hundred years ago in the kitchen of his Tijuana restaurant, low on ingredients, he invented the salad of crisp lettuce, croutons, eggs and anchovies that has borne his name ever since. Let us give thanks his parents didn't call him Kevin.*

This delightful version centres around crisp roast cauliflower rather than eggs (or the chicken that sometimes steps in) and leans on red miso and dulse where traditionally anchovies would add the dash of savoury. Dulse – a delicious dried seaweed – is now widely available; you can use crumbled nori sheets if you prefer.

*No offence Kevins, but you have to admit Kevin Salad carries little of the regal appeal of Caesar Salad.

Serves 4

1 medium cauliflower, cut into small florets

4 tbsp extra virgin olive oil

1 garlic clove, peeled

2 slices of sourdough or ciabatta, crusts removed and cut or torn into small pieces

2 romaine lettuces, washed, dried and roughly chopped

40g (1½oz) Parmesan cheese, shaved

flaky sea salt and freshly ground black pepper

cracked pink peppercorns or Aleppo chilli flakes, to serve

For the dressing

150g (5oz) mayonnaise

juice of ½ lemon

1 tsp Dijon mustard

1 garlic clove, crushed

2 tbsp dulse flakes, plus more for sprinkling

2 tbsp red miso

40g (1½oz) Parmesan cheese, finely grated

Preheat the oven to 220°C/200°C fan/425°F.

In a large bowl, toss the cauliflower florets with half the olive oil and some salt and pepper until well coated. Spread them out in a single layer on a baking sheet, then roast for about 15 minutes until golden and slightly crisp. Remove from the oven.

Heat the remaining 2 tablespoons olive oil in a frying pan with the garlic clove. Add the bread pieces and fry for 3–5 minutes until golden and crisp. Drain the bread on kitchen paper, discarding the garlic.

In a small bowl, whisk together the dressing ingredients and season with salt and pepper to taste.

Combine the lettuce, cauliflower and croutons in a large salad bowl. Toss with half the dressing to coat evenly, then drizzle over the rest. Scatter with the Parmesan shavings, a few more dulse flakes and some cracked pink peppercorns or Aleppo chilli flakes.

VEGAN: Use a plant-based mayo and cheese.
GF: Use GF bread.
SEASONAL SWAPS: Broccoli, asparagus and Jerusalem artichokes are among those that you might swap the cauliflower for.

SWEETCORN ROJAK

Rojaks are South East Asian salads, typically full of high-season vegetables, fruit, leaves and crunch, with sweet and sour in lively balance. There is nothing shy about a rojak. I eat variations on the theme whenever the sun is high (or I want the feeling it is). Frequently the result of taking its spirit to whatever is in the kitchen or is doing well in the garden takes it further from its spiritual home. No matter: if this leans towards Mexico and Spain as much as South East Asia, the flavour is compromised not one bit.

Kikos are fried, salted nuggets of sweetcorn, and very easily consumed with a cold one watching a match. If you can't find them locally or online, try crushed pistachios or Bombay mix.

Serves 4

1 tsp chilli flakes

1 tsp smoked paprika

1 tsp ground cumin

4 ears of sweetcorn, quartered lengthways

1 large red onion, sliced into rounds

300g (10oz) cherry tomatoes, whole

4 courgettes (zucchini), cut in half lengthways

2 tbsp extra virgin olive oil

2 limes: 1 juiced, 1 cut into wedges

small bunch of coriander (cilantro), finely chopped

100g (3½oz) kikos, partially crushed

flaky sea salt and freshly ground black pepper

For the tamarind dressing

3 tbsp tamarind paste

2 tsp brown sugar

juice of 2 limes

2 tbsp extra virgin olive oil

flaky sea salt and freshly ground black pepper

Preheat the grill (broiler) to a medium-high heat.

In a small bowl, mix together the chilli flakes, smoked paprika, ground cumin and some salt and pepper.

Brush the sweetcorn, onion, tomatoes and courgettes with the olive oil, place on a baking tray, and generously sprinkle the spice mixture over, coating evenly. Place under the grill and cook for about 8–10 minutes until they are charred and tender. Remove from the heat and squeeze over the lime juice.

Mix together all the ingredients for the dressing, then drizzle this over the grilled vegetables. Scatter with the coriander and kikos, with the lime wedges on the side.

VEGAN: Yes.
GF: Yes.
SEASONAL SWAPS: Treat this as a core recipe that you can play around with; make it as is so you get the feel of it, and as long as you keep the overall weight of vegetables the same, you can experiment as you like.

NEW SEASON TUMBLE

In the UK, we are lucky enough to enjoy Jersey Royal potatoes through spring. Grown on the island that gives them their name, the earliest harvest is lifted from the south-facing coastal slopes known as côtils. The soils are typically light and free-draining, the potatoes developing quickly in the sun. Delightful as these early Jerseys are, I prefer them a little later in the season – when the price has also dipped – as to my taste buds they have a deeper flavour, perhaps because they have grown more slowly. If Jersey Royal season has passed, any excellent new potato will work here very well too.

Dried limes are widely available in supermarkets now; these dark sun-dried limes are delightfully sour and set off the natural sweetness of the new season perfectly, but lemon will do a pretty fine job if you prefer.

Serves 4

800g (1lb 12oz) small new potatoes, skin on and scrubbed

45g (3 tbsp) butter or olive oil

bunch of spring onions (scallions), trimmed and cut into 4cm (1½in) pieces

big handful of wild garlic (or use a little crushed garlic)

300g (10oz) cooked peas

250g (9oz) cooked broad (fava) beans

2 tsp dried lime flakes or powder (or use lemon zest)

sea salt and freshly ground black pepper

Boil the potatoes in salted water for about 15–20 minutes until just cooked. Drain and keep warm.

Heat the butter or olive oil in a large pan over a medium heat and cook the spring onions for a minute or so, then stir in the wild garlic and cook until just wilted. Stir in the potatoes, peas and broad beans and season with salt and pepper. Serve sprinkled with the dried lime.

VEGAN: Yes.
GF: Yes.
SEASONAL SWAPS: Asparagus, thinly sliced red onions and green beans can all be used instead of the peas and broad beans.

SALAD OF BLUE CHEESE, SPROUTS + ARTICHOKES

With their deep, savoury, earthy flavour, Jerusalem artichokes are one of my favourite cold-weather vegetables. While not crisping like a potato when roasted, they kind of collapse just enough to take on any adjacent flavours; they also soften when simmered into an earthy, sweet purée that was made for this combination of brassica bitterness and the hint of sourness from the blue cheese. A proper treat.

Serves 4

350g (12oz) Jerusalem artichokes, scrubbed clean, peeled and diced (reserve the peels)

150ml (5fl oz) milk

a few sprigs of thyme, plus 2 tsp thyme leaves

4 tbsp olive oil, plus a little more for frying the skins

1 tsp harissa

400g (14oz) Brussels sprouts, thinly sliced

½ tbsp fennel seeds

big handful of sprout tops (optional, if available)

100g (3½oz) blue cheese, chopped into small pieces

50g (2oz) lightly toasted walnuts, roughly chopped

juice of ½ lemon

sea salt and freshly ground black pepper

Preheat the oven to 180°C/160°C fan/350°F.

Put the artichokes in a saucepan with the milk and 150ml (5fl oz) water, the thyme sprigs and a good pinch of salt. Bring to the boil, then reduce the heat and simmer for 15–20 minutes until the artichokes are tender. Drain and use a stick blender to blend the artichokes to a smooth purée, using a bit of the cooking liquid if required.

Meanwhile, brush the artichoke skins with a little olive oil and cook on a tray in the oven until crisp, about 7–10 minutes. Alternatively, heat a small frying pan with a generous glug of oil and fry the skins for 5 minutes until they turn brown and crisp, draining on kitchen paper. Season with a pinch of salt.

Combine 1 tablespoon of the olive oil with the harissa in a small bowl and set aside.

Fry the sprouts in the rest of the olive oil over a high heat, with a pinch of salt and the fennel seeds, for 5 minutes until the sprouts are softened and beginning to colour – do this in batches if required. If using sprout tops, quickly sauté in a little oil until slightly wilted and season with salt and pepper.

Spread the sprouts (and tops) over a platter, spoon over the artichoke purée, then dot with the blue cheese and walnuts. Finish by scattering over the artichoke skins and thyme leaves. Drizzle with the harissa oil, then squeeze over some lemon juice.

VEGAN: Use plant-based milk and cheese.
GF: Yes.
SEASONAL SWAPS: You can use celeriac instead of Jerusalem artichokes, whipped feta or tofu instead of the blue cheese, and shredded kale or pointy cabbage wedges instead of the sprouts.

A PERFECT SALAD

This is one of those rare combinations where each element makes every other element happier, and the comprehensiveness of their coming together means that there is nothing else that could be added to improve it. Sweet, sour, bitter, pungent and a joy of contrasting textures: for once, I unhumbly present 'a perfect salad'.

Serves 4

100g (3½oz) pitted prunes

2 tbsp sherry vinegar

90ml (6 tbsp) extra virgin olive oil, plus a bit more for drizzling

16 sage leaves

1 garlic clove, peeled and left whole

200g (7oz) rye bread, very thinly sliced, crusts removed and torn into small pieces

1 large radicchio, cored and roughly chopped

300g (10oz) burrata, drained

flaky sea salt and freshly ground black pepper

Put the prunes into a bowl with the vinegar and a pinch of salt and pepper.

Heat 3 tablespoons of the olive oil in a heavy-based frying pan over a medium heat and add the sage leaves. Cook until the sage bubbles and becomes crisp. Remove with a slotted spoon and drain on kitchen paper, returning the pan to the heat.

Add the garlic clove to the hot oil and stir well, then add the rye bread and fry, stirring often, until the bread turns golden and crisp. Using a slotted spoon, transfer the bread to a plate lined with kitchen paper and discard the garlic clove.

Toss the radicchio into the bowl of prunes and vinegar along with the remaining olive oil, adding a little more salt and pepper.

To serve, arrange the salad on a platter and tear the burrata over. Top with the sage leaves, the bread and a drizzle more oil.

VEGAN: Swap the burrata out for whatever plant-based cheese you fancy.
GF: Use GF bread.
SEASONAL SWAPS: Try swapping the radicchio for any other bitter leaf, although I do think the original iteration of this salad is the best.

HERBY CARROTS + PARSNIPS WITH PLUMS

The herbs and spice here are a classically Scandinavian combination and – as is so often the case – one of the reasons they go so well with the carrot and parsnip is that they belong to the same botanical family, *Apiaceae*. The plums bring delightful contrast in flavour and texture, somehow emphasizing both the earthiness and sweetness of the root vegetables. Keeping the spices and herbs separate until serving makes such a difference here; they remain distinct, each adding its character without being lost to the whole.

If the weather's warm, serve with a green salad; if chilly, shredded spring greens or broccoli will be perfect.

Serves 4

450g (1lb) carrots, peeled and halved lengthways

450g (1lb) parsnips, peeled and halved lengthways

2 onions, sliced into rings

4 tbsp extra virgin olive oil

2 tsp caraway seeds

6 plums, halved and stones removed

1 tbsp honey or brown sugar

1 tbsp red wine vinegar

2 tsp ground fennel

juice and grated zest of 1 small lemon

150g (5oz) yoghurt

small bunch of dill, roughly chopped

flaky sea salt and freshly ground black pepper

Preheat the oven to 200°C/180°C fan/400°F.

Put the carrots, parsnips and onions into a roasting tray, add 3 tablespoons of the olive oil and season with salt and pepper. Mix well, then cover tightly with foil and roast for about 30–35 minutes until tender. Stir in the caraway seeds and cook for 5 minutes more, uncovered.

While that's cooking, drizzle the plums with the remaining tablespoon of oil, the honey and vinegar and roast for 15 minutes or so until the plums are tender but still holding their shape.

Stir the fennel, a good twist of salt and pepper and a squeeze of lemon juice into the yoghurt.

Stir the remaining lemon juice and the zest into the vegetables and serve with the plums and yoghurt, with a scattering of dill over the top.

VEGAN: Coconut yoghurt works well here.
GF: Yes.
SEASONAL SWAPS: Try celeriac, beetroot (beet) and/or Jerusalem artichokes for the root vegetables, and peaches, apricots, grapes or blackberries (the latter barely cooked) instead of plums.

GREEN BEANS, BEETROOT, ORANGE + HAZELNUTS

As with the radicchio, prunes and burrata recipe on page 52, every single ingredient of this wonderful salad pairs beautifully with the rest. Nothing sits outside, there is no culinary third-cousin shipped in for contrary contrast, and yet it is delightfully balanced, wanting nothing. For variation, try using the parsley leaves whole as a salad leaf: much as I love it chopped, that fresh grassy, gentle bitterness works so well whole, especially with beetroot.

Serves 4

200g (7oz) natural yoghurt

3 tbsp tahini

1 garlic clove, crushed

1 tbsp sesame seeds

2 tsp cumin seeds

80g (3oz) hazelnuts, chopped

300g (10oz) green beans, trimmed and sliced

4 tbsp extra virgin olive oil

4–6 baby beetroots (beet), cooked, peeled and thinly sliced

2 oranges, peeled and thinly sliced (across the equator)

small bunch of parsley, leaves only, roughly chopped or left whole

2 tbsp red wine vinegar

flaky sea salt and freshly ground black pepper

Mix the yoghurt, tahini and garlic together and season with salt and pepper.

In a medium frying pan, dry-fry the sesame seeds, cumin seeds and hazelnuts for 1–2 minutes until fragrant.

Preheat the grill (broiler) to medium-high. Toss the green beans with 1 tablespoon of the olive oil and a big pinch of salt and grill for 1–2 minutes on each side until the beans are beginning to char and are tender but retain some crunch.

In a large salad bowl, combine the beetroot, orange slices and fresh parsley, then add the remaining olive oil and the vinegar. Season with salt and pepper to taste.

Spoon the yoghurt dressing onto the plate and arrange the salad and beans over the top, then sprinkle with the seeds and hazelnuts.

VEGAN: Use plant-based yoghurt.
GF: Yes.
SEASONAL SWAPS: Of the numerous variations that might work well, try any earthy root vegetable (parsnips, carrots etc.) instead of beetroot. Asparagus or runners can replace the green beans, while you can swap the orange for any other citrus. Walnuts or almonds would work instead of the hazelnuts.

Soups

PEA + PARSLEY SOUP

Although I love this most when summer has really arrived and the peas in the garden are perhaps too numerous to enjoy raw just as sweet treats, I'm really happy making this with frozen peas at any time of year. The extra edge you get with fresh peas is being able to add the pods to the vegetable stock with the parsley stalks; the result is a deeper pea flavour. If you have a lettuce or three, you can always wash, shred and add it to the mix at the same time as the peas for a differently wonderful, more grassy soup.

Serves 4

900ml (2 pints) vegetable stock (page 192, or use good shop-bought)

small bunch of parsley, leaves picked and finely chopped, stalks reserved

4 tbsp extra virgin olive oil

1 onion, finely chopped

2 garlic cloves, finely chopped

1.2kg (2lb 10oz) fresh or frozen peas

150ml (5fl oz) double (heavy) cream

flaky sea salt and freshly ground black pepper

crispy fried chickpeas, to serve

pea shoots, to serve (optional)

Bring the stock to the boil in a large pan, add the parsley stalks and put to one side to infuse.

Heat the olive oil in another large pan over a low-medium heat, add the onion and cook for about 10 minutes until soft, stirring frequently. Add the garlic and cook for 1 minute before adding the peas; cook for 2 minutes, stirring occasionally.

Strain in the vegetable stock, discarding the parsley stalks, and bring to a simmer. Reduce the heat to low, cover and simmer gently for about 5 minutes until the peas are tender. If using frozen peas, they may require a shorter cooking time.

Remove from the heat and add the parsley leaves. Blitz the soup in a food processor or blender – in batches if needed – until smooth. Return the soup to the pan, stir in the cream and season with salt and pepper to taste. Serve topped with crispy chickpeas and pea shoots, or parsley, as you prefer, and perhaps a splash more cream.

VEGAN: Use plant-based cream.
GF: Yes.
SEASONAL SWAPS: To be honest, peas are so good here that I'd concentrate the meddling on trying different herbs instead of the parsley, such as lovage, mint, chives and basil.

CHICKPEA + CABBAGE SOUP WITH PAPRIKA OIL

There is a day, somewhere between the ages of 39 and 47 (or about 2 months after the arrival of your first child, whichever comes first) where your primary ambitions move wholesale and unannounced from a fantasy life peppered with travel, adventure and outstanding sex frequently enjoyed, to the oasis of an easy midweek supper. Not only is this quick, nutritious and delicious, making a double batch also solves tomorrow night's tea. Winner winner, chickpea dinner.

This sustaining, deeply flavoursome soup is perfect for lunch as it is, but if you want it for an evening meal add a couple of slices of toast (rubbed with garlic if you have no plans for intimate relations). And if you make too much of that paprika oil, try it drizzled over fried eggs on toast in the morning.

Serves 4

90ml (6 tbsp) extra virgin olive oil

1 large onion, finely diced

2 bay leaves

5 garlic cloves, very thinly sliced

300g (10oz) white cabbage, cored and thinly sliced

500g (1lb 2oz) potatoes, peeled and cut into 2cm (¾in) dice

1 litre (2 pints) vegetable stock (page 192, or use good shop-bought)

1 tsp smoked paprika

1 tbsp red wine vinegar

2 x 400g (14oz) cans chickpeas, drained and rinsed

small bunch of parsley, finely chopped

flaky sea salt and freshly ground black pepper

Add half the olive oil to a heavy-based pan over a medium heat, followed by the onion and a good pinch of salt. Cook for 10 minutes, stirring often until the onion is soft. Add the bay leaves and half the garlic and cook for 1 minute. Add the cabbage and potatoes and cook for 5 minutes, stirring occasionally. Add the stock, taste and season with a little salt and pepper if you think it needs it, then simmer for 20 minutes until the potatoes are tender.

Meanwhile, in a small pan, heat the remaining garlic in the rest of the olive oil for a few minutes until it begins to bubble gently; watch closely until it just turns golden. Immediately remove the pan from the heat and stir in the paprika and vinegar.

Transfer a third of the soup to a blender and whizz until smooth, then return to the pan, along with the chickpeas and the parsley, and warm through.

Check the seasoning and tweak if necessary. Serve drizzled with the paprika oil.

VEGAN: Yes.
GF: Yes.
SEASONAL SWAPS: Sprouting broccoli, leeks, asparagus and chard are among the many vegetables you can use instead of the cabbage. Jerusalem artichokes or celeriac work really well in place of the potatoes.

SALMOREJO

There was a time when the idea of cold soup seemed as appealing as a fudge sandwich, and then gazpacho came round to tea one day. That cold Spanish soup – typically of tomatoes, cucumber and other summer vegetables – is a marvellous thing, and this wonderful Andalusian cold soup – a classically simpler affair of tomatoes, pepper and stale bread – is its equal. It originated as height-of-summer cheap food, using old bread and what was plentiful – check the similarity of core ingredients with Italy's panzanella (page 26) – and as is so often the case when imaginatively using only what you have, the results are life-enhancing.

At the risk of sounding like a broken record, the simplicity of this gives ordinary ingredients nowhere to hide: use as good as you can and you'll taste it.

Serves 4

1kg (2lb 4oz) ripe tomatoes

1 red pepper, deseeded

100g (3½oz) sourdough bread (a day or two old), crusts removed

100ml (3½fl oz) extra virgin olive oil, plus extra for drizzling

2 garlic cloves, thinly sliced

1 green pepper, deseeded and chopped

1 tbsp sherry vinegar, plus more to taste

flaky sea salt

To serve

2 hard-boiled eggs, finely chopped

30g (1oz) smoked almonds, thinly sliced

30g (1oz) green olives, finely chopped

Preheat the oven to 200°C/180°C fan/400°F.

Put the tomatoes and red pepper into a tray and roast for 20 minutes until tender. Allow to cool slightly, then peel the pepper and tomatoes, removing as much skin as you can.

Meanwhile, put the bread into a bowl with the olive oil and 50ml (2fl oz) cold water and leave to soak for 5 minutes.

Put the garlic, cooled tomatoes and pepper into a food processor or blender with the soaked bread and oil, green pepper and sherry vinegar and blitz until very smooth. Season to taste with salt and more vinegar. Chill for at least an hour.

Serve with the egg, almonds and olives scattered on top, and drizzle with a little more oil.

VEGAN: Omit the eggs.
GF: Use GF bread.
SEASONAL SWAPS: You can make this completely raw by submerging the tomatoes and peppers in boiling water for a few minutes, then removing and discarding the now cooperative skins: the result is lighter and absolutely fabulous, but roasting intensifies the flavour and I often prefer it this way. The choice is yours.

SUMMER MINESTRONE

When the garden – or the market – is full of summer vegetables, this Italian soup is where you should turn. Upholstered by pasta and beans, this celebration of the garden relies on the freshness of its ingredients and the cook's attention: taste regularly, seasoning as needed, as you go.

Tradition has it that minestrone embellished with pistou changes the designation of the soup to match the name of this nutless pesto, but I'm attached to the word 'minestrone'. A childhood spent frequently eating a canned version has rendered it delicious in my memory (I shall not risk disappointment by tasting it in middle age).

Serves 4

80g (3oz) little pasta shapes (or use risotto rice)

4 tbsp extra virgin olive oil, plus more to coat the pasta

1 onion, finely chopped

1 medium fennel bulb, trimmed and finely chopped

1 large carrot, very finely chopped

2 garlic cloves, finely chopped

150g (5oz) chard, leaves cut into ribbons, stalks finely chopped

2 bay leaves

4 large ripe tomatoes, peeled, deseeded and finely chopped

300g (10oz) green beans, cut into 2cm (¾in) pieces

2–3 firm courgettes (zucchini), finely chopped

900ml (2 pints) vegetable stock (page 192, or use good shop-bought)

400g (14oz) can borlotti or cannellini beans, drained and rinsed

flaky sea salt and freshly ground black pepper

For the pistou

50g (2oz) basil leaves

1 garlic clove, finely chopped

75ml (5 tbsp) extra virgin olive oil

30g (1¼oz) pecorino or Parmesan cheese, finely grated

Cook the pasta shapes following the instructions on the packet until al dente. Drain, rinse with cold water and coat with a little oil to prevent the pasta from clumping together.

Place all the ingredients for the pistou in a pestle and mortar or in a blender and pulse until smooth. Taste and season with salt and pepper.

Heat the olive oil in a pan over a low-medium heat and cook the onion, fennel and carrot for about 15 minutes until very soft and beginning to stick to the pan. Add the garlic, chard stalks and bay leaves and cook for 1 minute. Add the tomatoes, green beans and courgettes and cook for 2–3 minutes until thickened.

Pour in the vegetable stock and bring to the boil, then add the chard leaves, the cooked pasta and the drained beans. Cook for 2 minutes until piping hot and the chard is wilted. Taste and season with salt and pepper if needed.

Remove the bay leaves and serve in bowls with a big spoonful of the pistou on top.

VEGAN: Use a plant-based hard cheese.
GF: Use GF pasta.
SEASONAL SWAPS: Make a differently superb winter approximation with canned tomatoes, shredded kale and/or more chard in place of the courgettes.

ASPARAGUS SOUP WITH POACHED EGGS + CRISP SHALLOTS

There is a point in late spring when asparagus goes from super expensive to just a little pricey; until that point I want asparagus just as it is – barely boiled – but once that threshold is crossed I start thinking about this soup. You can, of course, make asparagus soup using just the tough part of the stem, but this uses each part – the tips, tough stalk and succulent stem – to the most beautiful effect. The poached egg brings creamy delight and turns this into a main meal, while the shallots bring texture and contrast.

Serves 4

vegetable oil, for frying

8 large shallots, thinly sliced

1 litre (2 pints) vegetable stock (page 192, or use good shop-bought)

1–2 bunches of asparagus, tough ends removed and reserved, tips reserved, stems thinly sliced

2 leeks, trimmed and thinly sliced (keep the leek peelings)

2 tbsp extra virgin olive oil

1 tbsp butter

2 tbsp white vinegar

4 eggs

flaky sea salt and freshly ground black pepper

Heat the vegetable oil in a small pan over a medium heat until the temperature reaches 180°C (350°F) – when you lower a piece of shallot into the oil it should sizzle immediately. Add three-quarters of the shallots and fry, carefully stirring often, for 2–4 minutes until golden and crisp. Remove the shallots using a slotted spoon (reserving the oil to be strained when cool for later use – it's perfect for frying potatoes and eggs in) and transfer to a plate lined with kitchen paper. Season with salt.

Bring the stock to a simmer in a large, deep pan and add the tough asparagus ends and leek peelings. Season to taste and allow to infuse.

Heat the olive oil and butter in a pan over a medium heat and cook the leeks and the rest of the shallots for 8 minutes or so until the onion has softened. Add the sliced asparagus stems and season with salt and pepper.

Strain the stock through a sieve into the pan (discarding the leek peelings and tough asparagus ends) and bring to the boil, then reduce the heat and simmer for 5 minutes. Blend the soup until completely smooth. Place over a low-medium heat to warm through again.

Bring 3 litres of water to a simmer in a deep pan and add the asparagus tips. Boil for 1–2 minutes until tender, then remove with a slotted spoon. Add the vinegar to the water and bring back to a simmer. Add the eggs one by one and poach for 3 minutes. Remove with a slotted spoon.

Pour the soup into four bowls and lower a poached egg into each one. Top with the asparagus tips, some black pepper and the crisp shallots and serve immediately with excellent bread.

VEGAN: Omit the poached egg and serve with bread.
GF: Yes (serve with GF bread).
SEASONAL SWAPS: Sprouting broccoli, tenderstem broccoli and peas are among the many vegetables you can switch in for the asparagus.

JERUSALEM ARTICHOKE + LEEK SOUP

Jerusalem artichokes – or sunchokes – and nutmeg were made to be together. The earthy sweetness of the artichokes, complemented by the oniony sweetness of the leeks falls perfectly into nutmeg's warm embrace. I've tried numerous variations on this – a little of celery's beautiful bitterness, or a scratch or two of lemon zest – but the more I leave out the better this tastes, so here it is in all its simplicity.

Serves 4

3 tbsp extra virgin olive oil

1 onion, sliced

2 leeks, thinly sliced

400g (14oz) Jerusalem artichokes, peeled and cut into 2cm (¾in) pieces

3 garlic cloves, chopped

1 litre (2 pints) vegetable stock (page 192, or use good shop-bought)

100ml (3½fl oz) double (heavy) cream

a good sprig of fresh thyme, leaves only

freshly grated nutmeg

4 tbsp finely chopped hazelnuts

flaky sea salt and freshly ground black pepper

Heat the olive oil in a large heavy-based pan over a low-medium heat, add the onion and leeks and cook for 10 minutes until softened. Add the artichokes, garlic and ½ teaspoon salt and cook for 5 minutes. Add the stock, cream, thyme leaves and more salt to taste. Simmer for 15–20 minutes until the artichokes are tender, stirring occasionally.

Blitz in a food processor or blender until smooth – in batches if necessary – adding salt, pepper and a generosity of nutmeg. Serve scattered with the hazelnuts and another good scratch of nutmeg.

VEGAN: Use plant-based cream.
GF: Yes.
SEASONAL SWAPS: This works beautifully with other root vegetables, especially parsnips (see the ice cream on page 211 for another of its perfect pairings with nutmeg).

WATERCRESS SOUP

My parents-in-law lived in that part of Hampshire that is bisected with rivers clear as gin, where trout as speckled as Woodstock t-shirts hold their position into the flow, gills wide, in search of sustenance. A short walk from their old house is one of the watercress beds where exactly this clarity of running water – purified by the semi-porous chalk through which it flows – is required to produce the lushest watercress. A few years ago, they relocated, but the taste of this bright and lightly punchy soup reminds me of those rolling chalk landscapes and the taste of the hoppiest of ales in the nearby pub as clearly as if I was there.

Serves 4

60ml (4 tbsp) extra virgin olive oil

2 leeks, trimmed, washed and thinly sliced

2 slices of sourdough bread, torn into bite-sized pieces

2 garlic cloves, finely chopped

500g (1lb 2oz) potatoes, peeled and diced

1 litre (2 pints) vegetable stock (page 192, or use good shop-bought)

about 150g (5oz) watercress

75ml (3fl oz) double (heavy) cream

flaky sea salt and freshly ground black pepper

Preheat the oven to 180°C/160°C fan/350°F.

Heat half the olive oil in a heavy-based pan over a medium heat, add the leeks and cook for 8–10 minutes, stirring occasionally, until the leeks are completely soft and translucent.

Meanwhile, put the sourdough on a baking tray and drizzle with the remaining olive oil. Toast in the oven until golden brown and crunchy, turning when needed.

Add the garlic and ½ teaspoon salt to the leeks and cook for 1 minute, then add the potatoes and stock and bring to the boil. Reduce the heat and simmer for 15–20 minutes until the potatoes are cooked. Add all but a small handful of watercress and half the cream and cook for 1–2 minutes until the watercress wilts but still retains its colour.

Season to taste with salt and pepper, then blend until smooth.

Serve in bowls topped with the croutons, a drizzle of the remaining cream and the reserved watercress.

VEGAN: Use plant-based cream.
GF: Use GF bread.
SEASONAL SWAPS: Lettuce, rocket (arugula) and peas (and indeed pea shoots) all make great variations.

RIBOLLITA

There is not a month, week or day that I am not overjoyed to eat ribollita; even in the height of summer, the sun pouring down, I'll happily raise a sweat with my spoon pecking into a bowl of this. It might be the most adaptable of all soups: in my time during the early days at River Cottage, there were endless versions of what we called Half the Garden Soup. I love this thick and glossy, but do feel free to add a little water or stock if needed as the bread cooks in.

Serves 4

4 tbsp extra virgin olive oil, plus more for drizzling

1 large onion, finely diced

1 large carrot, finely diced

4 celery sticks, finely diced

2 tsp fresh rosemary, finely chopped

3 garlic cloves, finely chopped

¼ tsp dried chilli flakes (optional)

400g (14oz) can chopped tomatoes

bunch of cavolo nero or kale, stalks removed and leaves thinly sliced

400g (14oz) can borlotti beans, drained and rinsed

900ml (2 pints) vegetable stock (page 192, or use good shop-bought)

2 thick slices of sourdough, crusts removed, toasted and roughly chopped

freshly grated Parmesan

flaky sea salt and freshly ground black pepper

Heat the olive oil in a large, heavy-based pan over a low-medium heat and cook the diced vegetables, stirring occasionally, for a good 10–15 minutes until very soft and only just starting to colour. Add the rosemary, garlic and chilli flakes (if using) and cook for another 2–3 minutes. Add the chopped tomatoes and cook for 10 minutes until thickened.

In a separate pan, cook the kale in boiling salted water for 3–5 minutes until tender, then drain.

Add the beans and the vegetable stock to the tomato pan and bring to the boil. Reduce the heat to low, add a big pinch of salt, the wilted kale and the bread and simmer, partially covered, for 10–15 minutes.

Taste and season, if needed. Divide among bowls and top with a little additional olive oil. Serve with grated Parmesan.

VEGAN: Omit the Parmesan.
GF: Use GF bread.
SEASONAL SWAPS: If you have no kale, use chard; the borlottis can be butter (lima) beans or cannellini beans, etc. This soup can and should represent what's good in your garden or the market at the time.

R

ice and
grains

TOMATO + CHERRY QUINOA WITH PISTACHIOS

This simple recipe – a seriously good celebration of high summer – deserves the very best tomatoes you can find. A mix of size, colour and flavour works really well, but if you have a bowlful of one excellent variety such as Gardeners' Delight or Honeycomb, don't hesitate.
The quick-pickled shallots are a wonderful thing: make them once and you'll find any number of uses to which to put them.

Serves 4

2 shallots, very thinly sliced
zest and juice of 1 lemon
150g (5oz) quinoa
6 tbsp extra virgin olive oil
400g (14oz) ripe tomatoes, sliced
200g (7oz) ripe cherries, pitted
80g (3oz) shelled pistachios
small bunch of fresh mint, leaves shredded
flaky sea salt and freshly ground black pepper

Mix the shallots with the lemon juice and leave for 5 minutes.

Boil the quinoa in a large pan of salted water for 12–15 minutes until tender, then drain well.

Spread the quinoa over a large serving platter and drizzle with half the olive oil. Arrange the tomatoes and cherries on top, sprinkle over the lemon zest and season with salt and pepper. Scatter with the shallots and lemon juice, followed by the pistachios and mint. Drizzle the remaining olive oil over the salad to serve.

VEGAN: Yes.
GF: Yes.
SEASONAL SWAPS: Roasted carrots and parsnips or fennel and beetroot (beet) make for superb winter variations instead of the tomatoes and cherries.

SUMMER INTO AUTUMN PILAF

There is a very good chance that wherever you are in the world, there will be a version of pilaf not far from you. Vegetables and rice cooked in stock, often in the presence of sweet and earthy spices, is very easy to love and – equally importantly – highly nutritious and easy to make.

Master this recipe and tweak it to the seasons: perhaps courgettes in summer, asparagus and broad (fava) beans in late spring and so on.

Serves 4

75g (2½oz) butter

1 small pointed cabbage, cut into wedges

200g (7oz) runner beans, trimmed and sliced

2 onions, thinly sliced

3 garlic cloves, thinly sliced

10 whole allspice berries

1 cinnamon stick

2 bay leaves

2 tsp ground cumin

2 tsp ground coriander

3 tbsp Turkish pepper paste (or use 2 tbsp tomato purée/paste with 2 tsp paprika)

300g (10oz) bulgur wheat, soaked in boiling water for 10 minutes and drained

800ml (1¾ pints) vegetable stock (page 192, or use good shop-bought), or water

1 lemon: ½ thinly sliced, ½ cut into wedges

80g (3oz) walnuts, roughly chopped

1–2 pinches of chilli flakes

small bunch of dill, finely chopped

flaky sea salt and freshly ground black pepper

Heat half the butter in a frying pan until it is foaming. Add the cabbage wedges and beans with a large pinch of salt and cook for about 10 minutes, turning often, until they have taken on some colour.

In a wide pan over a medium heat, cook the onions in the remaining butter for 10 minutes, stirring occasionally, until softened. Add the garlic, spices and pepper paste and cook for 1 minute. Stir in the bulgur wheat, pour in the stock and bring to the boil.

Add the half-cooked vegetables and the lemon slices and simmer uncovered over a low heat for 10–15 minutes until the bulgur and cabbage are tender and the stock has been absorbed.

Meanwhile, toast the walnuts in a dry frying pan, flipping often, until they are fragrant.

Spoon the pilaf onto a serving platter or individual plates, scatter with the walnuts, chilli flakes and dill, and serve with the lemon wedges on the side for squeezing.

VEGAN: Use olive oil instead of butter.
GF: Use buckwheat or quinoa instead of the bulgur wheat.
SEASONAL SWAPS: Cooler-weather versions of this are so good – try shredded sprouts, asparagus, roasted root vegetables and sprouting broccoli in place of the runner beans and cabbage.

RISI E BISI

This Venetian springtime wonder is favoured by some served as a stiff porridge; others prefer it runny like a thick soup. I like it needing the edges of a bowl to stop it walking out the door. Traditionally eaten to celebrate the feast of San Marco in late April, using the earliest of small, sweet peas, I have to wait until a month or so later in the UK climate for that pleasure, but it really is worth the anticipation. The fresher the peas, the better; the smaller, the sweeter. As you can tell by the proportion of peas to rice, this really is all about the peas. You can make a perfectly pleasurable – and, without the podding, quicker – version using frozen peas, and there really is a place for that, but if you want to make this at its absolute peak, use the best of spring's early peas and homemade stock.

Serves 4

1 litre (2 pints) vegetable stock (page 192, or use good shop-bought)

450g (1lb) podded fresh peas, pea pods reserved (or use defrosted frozen peas)

80g (3oz) butter

1 onion, finely chopped

1 leek, white part only, finely chopped

2 celery sticks, finely chopped

1 garlic clove, finely chopped

200g (7oz) risotto rice (arborio, Carnaroli, Vialone Nano)

freshly grated Parmesan, to serve

small bunch of parsley, finely chopped

flaky sea salt and freshly ground black pepper

Bring the stock to a simmer in a medium pan and add the pea pods, then turn the heat down very low.

Melt two-thirds of the butter in a large pan over a medium heat. Add the onion, leek, celery and garlic and cook for about 10 minutes until soft. Add the rice, stirring to toast the grains for 2–3 minutes.

Remove and discard the pods from the stock, and add 2 ladles of stock to the rice. Stir continuously until all the liquid has evaporated, then repeat with another 2 ladlefuls of stock, stirring until evaporated. Continue in this vein until all of the stock is used up. Check the rice continuously from about 15 minutes in; the grains should be tender but with a little bite.

Add the peas to the pan and continue to cook for another couple of minutes until the rice is just cooked.

Remove the pan from the heat and stir in a generous handful of Parmesan, the parsley and the remaining butter; season to taste with salt and pepper. Serve immediately, with more Parmesan to hand.

VEGAN: Use plant-based cheese and butter.
GF: Yes.
SEASONAL SWAPS: Make this as is, but when fresh peas are out of season, use frozen.

FREEKEH WITH SQUASH, BEETROOT + POMEGRANATE

This layering of vegetables, torn pitta, pomegranate seeds and yoghurt owes much to the Middle Eastern dish fatteh, though the absence of chickpeas and tahini take it just far enough from the authentic to test its elastic limit. If you have barley, spelt or quinoa, do try those in place of the freekeh which comes from green wheat – if you prefer. You can use shop-bought crispy onions, but to make your own, thinly slice a couple of onions, dredge them in a little cornflour (cornstarch) and deep-fry for 5 minutes or so until golden, then drain on kitchen paper.

Serves 4

200g (7oz) freekeh, rinsed

600g (1lb 5oz) butternut squash, peeled and cubed

400g (14oz) beetroot (beet), peeled and cubed

1 tsp fennel seeds

4 tbsp extra virgin olive oil, plus more to drizzle

150g (5oz) pitta bread, torn into bite-sized pieces

300g (10oz) Greek yoghurt

1 garlic clove, crushed

3 tbsp pomegranate molasses

50g (2oz) crispy fried onions

2 tbsp pine nuts

small bunch of flat-leaf parsley, finely chopped

1 pomegranate, seeds only

flaky sea salt and freshly ground black pepper

Preheat the oven to 200°C/180°C fan/400°F.

Boil the freekeh in a large pan of salted water for about 30–35 minutes until tender, then drain.

Toss the butternut squash and beetroot with the fennel seeds, olive oil and some salt and pepper. Spread out on a baking tray and roast for 25–30 minutes, or until tender and lightly coloured.

Toast the pitta bread in the oven for 5–8 minutes until crisp.

In a medium bowl, mix together the yoghurt and crushed garlic and season with salt and pepper.

To assemble, scatter half of the toasted pitta bread pieces in a serving dish. Spread half of the cooked freekeh on top, followed by half of the roasted squash and beetroot. Drizzle with some of the garlic yoghurt. Repeat the layering, then drizzle with the pomegranate molasses and a little olive oil. Top with the crispy onions, pine nuts, parsley and pomegranate seeds.

VEGAN: Use coconut (or other plant-based) yoghurt.
GF: Use GF pittas and ensure the crispy fried onions are GF.
SEASONAL SWAPS: The squash and beetroot can be substituted for whichever seasonal vegetables take your fancy: other roots such as parsnips and carrots, summer pairings that won't need roasting like artichoke hearts and tomatoes, or sprouting broccoli with chickpeas are a few of my favourites.

DOUBLE KALE TABBOULEH

If you have yet to fall in love with kale, this might just be the bunch of flowers you were looking for. While it is perfectly delightful steamed or briefly boiled, I love kale best either oiled and roasted until crisp, or raw, with a salt rub letting the texture down just enough to please the bite. Make this and I'm confident that not only will this recipe become a winter favourite, you'll also be taking these two ways of preparing kale into so many other meals.

This tabbouleh is a miracle in itself, taking the brightest of winter's vegetables – fennel, kale, cauliflower – and sliding them into something that looks hard out of the window at summer without ever leaving the comfort of the house.

Serves 4

150g (5oz) coarse bulgur wheat

200g (7oz) curly kale, stalks removed

2 tbsp extra virgin olive oil

1 tbsp sesame seeds

1 fennel bulb, trimmed and finely chopped

½ small cauliflower, trimmed of leaves and shaved into tiny florets (a mandoline is helpful here)

1 large pomegranate, seeds only

50g (2oz) dried pear, thinly sliced

small bunch of flat-leaf parsley, roughly chopped

50g (2oz) lightly toasted walnuts, roughly chopped

1 tsp sumac, plus more to sprinkle on top

juice of ½ lemon

flaky sea salt and freshly ground black pepper

For the dressing

zest and juice of ½ lemon

80ml (3fl oz) olive oil

50ml (2fl oz) pomegranate molasses

1 small garlic clove, crushed

½ tsp ground cinnamon

Preheat the oven to 160°C/140°C fan/320°F and line a baking tray with baking parchment.

Soak the bulgur according to the packet instructions, then drain in a sieve, refresh with cold water and drain well.

Tear half the kale leaves into roughly 3–4cm (1¼–1½in) pieces and toss with the olive oil, a pinch of salt and the sesame seeds. Arrange in a single layer on the baking tray and cook for 4–8 minutes, giving a couple of stirs, until crisp and dark green with a little brown at the edges.

Thinly slice the rest of the kale, rub vigorously with a good pinch of salt (this seasons and also softens the texture) and stir into the bulgur.

Mix all of the dressing ingredients and season to taste, then mix into the bulgur with all of the remaining ingredients (except the roasted kale) and check the seasoning. Stir through half the roasted kale and spread the tabbouleh out on a platter, topping with the remaining roasted kale and a sprinkle of sumac.

VEGAN: Yes.

GF: Use buckwheat or quinoa instead of the bulgur wheat.

SEASONAL SWAPS: The vegetables in this recipe are available all year, so you can make this whenever the mood takes, but don't let that stop you substituting other vegetables to a roughly equal weight.

CHICORY, BEETROOT + TALEGGIO WITH POLENTA

This is such a simple yet satisfying combination of beetroot's sweetness and chicory's bitterness, with a little gentle sourness from the cheese. Delicious as this is, the three main ingredients are readily substitutable, but do keep that balance of flavours in mind: for example, if you switch out chicory for little gems, you can bring a little bitterness by swapping celeriac for the beetroot.

Serves 4

6 medium beetroot (beet)

900ml (2 pints) vegetable stock (page 192, or use good shop-bought) or water

150g (5oz) coarse polenta

50g (2oz) grated Parmesan

50g (2oz) butter, diced

1 tbsp extra virgin olive oil

4 chicory (endive), halved lengthways, quartered if large

60g (2¼oz) walnuts, roughly chopped

150g (5oz) taleggio, or another semi-soft cheese, sliced

small bunch of flat-leaf parsley, roughly chopped

flaky sea salt and freshly ground black pepper

Preheat the oven to 200°C/180°C fan/400°F.

Wrap the beetroot in a double layer of foil and roast for 30–40 minutes until tender. Allow to cool until they are cool enough to peel, then cut in half.

Bring the stock to a simmer in a large pan. Pour in the polenta in a thin stream, whisking constantly to prevent lumps. Once incorporated, use a wooden spoon to stir constantly for 5 minutes as it cooks. Turn the heat down low and continue to cook gently for 15–20 minutes, giving it a vigorous stir every couple of minutes. Remove from the heat and stir in the Parmesan and butter, then cover and leave somewhere warm.

Heat the olive oil in a frying pan over a medium heat and fry the chicory with a generous pinch of salt until just wilted and beginning to brown. Add the chopped walnuts and give them a couple of minutes in the pan – stirring occasionally – to warm through.

Spoon the polenta onto each plate, dot with the taleggio, and arrange the beetroot, chicory, walnuts and the parsley as you like. Season with salt and pepper.

VEGAN: Use plant-based butter and cheese.
GF: Yes.
SEASONAL SWAPS: Try other root vegetables, squash or courgettes (zucchini) instead of beetroot; and roasted kale, chard or little gem quarters in place of the chicory.

AUBERGINE KEDGEREE

Classically made with smoked fish, kedgeree is also wonderful made with aubergines, where the smokiness from their cooking enters into the holiest of alliances with the spices and the egg. Embellish this as you like – handfuls of peas, slices of briefly fried courgette (zucchini) – but the simplicity here is such a joy.

Serves 4

2 large aubergines (eggplants)

1 tsp garam masala

2 eggs

300g (10oz) basmati rice

3 tbsp butter (or oil)

1 onion, finely chopped

1½ tbsp curry powder

450ml (1 pint) vegetable stock (page 192, or use good shop-bought) or water

small bunch of coriander (cilantro), finely chopped

1–2 green chillies, thinly sliced

2 lemons, cut into wedges

flaky sea salt and freshly ground black pepper

Begin by cooking the aubergines. You can do this by placing them on a baking tray under a hot grill, on the barbecue or – as I usually do – directly over a gas flame on the stovetop. Use tongs to turn them occasionally until the skin is charred and the flesh completely tender. Remove from the heat, cut a slit with a knife and place them cut-side down in a colander to drain away their juice as they cool.

When cooled a little, lay them on a chopping board and open each aubergine like a butterfly, spooning out the flesh and pulling it into long strips. Season with salt and pepper and the garam masala. Discard the skin, though don't worry about a few flecks in with the flesh, as they bring a touch of welcome bitter smokiness.

Put the eggs into a large pan of salted water and bring to the boil. From boiling, cook for 8 minutes, then scoop out and cool in cold water. Peel and halve each egg.

Rinse the basmati rice under cold water until the water runs clear, then drain well.

Melt the butter in a medium frying pan over a medium heat, add the onion and cook for 10 minutes until softened, then add the curry powder, stirring well, and cook for about 1 minute until fragrant. Pour in the vegetable stock and bring to a simmer, adding salt and a good grinding of pepper. Add the rice, cover and cook for 15–20 minutes until tender. Allow it to rest for 5 minutes.

Turn the rice out onto a platter and fluff the rice with a fork, folding the chopped boiled eggs and the roasted aubergines through. Scatter with coriander and sliced chilli and serve with lemon wedges to the side.

VEGAN: There's no similar substitute for the eggs, but a few handfuls of cooked chickpeas, fried in a little oil, salt and garam masala works differently well.
GF: Yes.
SEASONAL SWAPS: The smokiness and texture of the aubergines is unique, but – however differently – this works beautifully with sweet potatoes (bake them in the oven), or for a more complete change try steamed tenderstem broccoli, strips of cooked (bell) pepper (jarred are excellent), and/or cooked globe artichoke hearts.

RADICCHIO + CHESTNUT RISOTTO

I had given up on risotto. It's not that I didn't like it well enough, it just seemed like an awful lot of standing and stirring for a whole lot of okayness. Then I accidentally* ate risotto made by Raymond Blanc and it is one of only two meals** I have placed my fork down after a mouthful and reconsidered the nature of the universe and my place in it.

As is so often the case, the little things turn out to be the big: quality of ingredients (especially the stock), adding the liquid in instalments, stirring with continuity, allowing it to rest off the heat before stirring in the butter and cheese and the texture contrast of the topping make all the difference.

*I'll bore you with that story should we ever be in the same place.
**I'll bore you with the other should you still be stood there after the first story.

Serves 4

1 small radicchio: ¾ roughly chopped, ¼ thinly sliced

15 peeled chestnuts, roughly chopped

2 tbsp extra virgin olive oil

1 tsp thyme leaves

2 tbsp red wine vinegar

40g (1½oz) butter

1 small white onion, very finely diced

2 celery sticks, very finely diced

400g (14oz) risotto rice (arborio, Carnaroli, Vialone Nano)

175ml (6fl oz) dry red wine (about 1 glass)

1 litre (2 pints) hot vegetable stock (page 192, or use good shop-bought)

80g (3oz) Parmesan, grated

flaky sea salt and freshly ground black pepper

Preheat the oven to 200°C/180°C fan/400°F and line a baking tray with baking parchment.

Mix the roughly chopped radicchio and chestnuts with half the olive oil, the thyme leaves, vinegar and a good pinch of salt and pepper. Place on the lined tray and roast in the oven for 10–15 minutes, stirring a couple of times until it is tender and beginning to caramelize.

While the radicchio is cooking, melt half the butter over a medium heat in a large, heavy-based pan and stir in the rest of the olive oil. Add the onion and celery and cook for 10 minutes until soft and translucent. Stir in the rice and ½ teaspoon salt, turning the heat up slightly and stirring for a minute to toast and coat the grains.

Add the wine and cook while stirring until all the wine has evaporated. Reduce the heat back to medium and add the first ladleful of hot stock. Stir continuously until all the liquid has evaporated, then repeat with another ladleful of stock, stirring until evaporated. Add the thinly sliced radicchio after 10 minutes. Continue to add a ladleful at a time, stirring constantly, until all of the stock is used up.

Check the rice from about 15 minutes in; you want the grains to be tender but with a little bite. When the rice is ready, remove from the heat and beat in the remaining butter and half the Parmesan. Check the seasoning, cover and allow it to rest for 2 minutes.

Serve topped with the roasted radicchio and take the remaining Parmesan to the table for people to add their own.

VEGAN: Use plant-based butter and cheese to finish.
GF: Yes.
SEASONAL SWAPS: Risotto might be the ultimate four-seasons food, using the best of what is at its peak. Tomatoes, grated beetroot (beet), asparagus, peas, broad (fava) beans, grated parsnips and so many others…

Pasta

SUMMER PASTA SALAD

When the sun shines hard and you fancy pasta but nothing hot, this is the recipe to turn to. With the combination of dried fruit, pine nuts, capers and olives, and the gentle sense of sweet and sour, this leans hard towards Sicily. It's so good as a side for a couple of roast chickens when you have a large tableful of guests, but plenty delightful enough to make a fine midweek main with a leafy side. It is highly adaptable, but one thing I'd keep constant is a short twisted pasta: if it resembles Brian May's hair/guitar lead, so much the better to catch the sauce.

Serves 4

20g (¾oz) basil, leaves picked

2 garlic cloves, peeled

200g (7oz) cherry tomatoes, cut in half

60ml (4 tbsp) extra virgin olive oil

finely grated zest and juice of 1 small orange

finely grated zest and juice of 1 lemon

400g (14oz) short pasta

40g (1½oz) currants or raisins

3 tbsp capers

80g (3oz) black olives, roughly chopped

40g (1½oz) pine nuts

small bunch of fennel fronds, roughly chopped

flaky sea salt and freshly ground black pepper

Blend the basil with the garlic, half the tomatoes and the olive oil. Stir in the zest and juice of the orange and lemon.

Cook the pasta in a large pan of boiling salted water according to the packet instructions, or until al dente; drain and tip into a bowl.

Stir the dressing and currants through the pasta and allow to cool. Add the rest of the tomatoes, the capers, olives and pine nuts, and season to taste with salt and pepper. Scatter over the fennel fronds before serving.

VEGAN: Yes.
GF: Use GF pasta.
SEASONAL SWAPS: Try adding a handful of chopped courgettes, or replacing the currants with dried apricots, the fennel fronds for parsley, the citrus for red wine vinegar, and so on.

RUNNER BEAN PASTA WITH GRAPES + GOAT'S CHEESE

I have been somewhat evangelical about runner beans these last twenty years. Once I started growing my own and was able to pick the best varieties at their peak, I realized that – like strawberries, early peas and cherry tomatoes – they are best enjoyed raw, within touching distance of the plant that bore them. Get them rigid, glassy and crisp and they are as good as the best asparagus. Any I don't eat like that likely as not fall into this delight. Roast grapes really are something. If they are new to you in that form, do try this – I know you'll love it; set against the succulent, sweet beans, the chalky sourness of the cheese and the zip of the herb, the grapes sing beautifully.

Serves 4

300g (10oz) black grapes

4 tbsp extra virgin olive oil, plus extra for drizzling

400g (14oz) short pasta, such as casarecce or macaroni

300g (10oz) runner beans, trimmed and thinly sliced

100g (3½oz) soft goat's cheese, crumbled

small bunch of fresh fennel or dill fronds, chopped

flaky sea salt and freshly ground black pepper

Preheat the oven to 200°C/180°C/400°F.

Place the grapes on a baking sheet. Drizzle with the olive oil, season with salt and pepper and toss to coat evenly. Roast the grapes in the centre of the oven for about 15–20 minutes until the grapes are collapsing and releasing juices.

Cook the pasta in a large pan of salted water according to the package instructions, or until al dente, adding the runner beans for the last 4 minutes. Drain and return to the pan, reserving a little of the cooking water. Add the roasted grapes and any juices, the goat's cheese and chopped fennel or dill. Drizzle with a little more olive oil and toss to combine all the ingredients, seasoning with salt and pepper to taste.

VEGAN: Use plant-based cheese.
GF: Use GF pasta.
SEASONAL SWAPS: Do try this with asparagus in spring. The first of summer's green beans and roasted gooseberries in place of the grapes is really something.

DOUBLE FENNEL + OLIVE ORECCHIETTE

Pangrattato – what a gorgeous word – is one of those things that elevates wherever it is employed. It means 'grated bread', which is then fried in olive oil in the presence of garlic. It brings flavour and a most welcome crunch and you'll find yourself using it to turn a perfectly welcome Wednesday night dish into something special, for almost no effort.

Fennel is one of the vegetables many of us love but perhaps don't have many recipes for; this one is so good and I'm pretty sure will become a favourite if you give it a go.

One of the secrets to getting this just right is nailing the consistency: it should be generously glossy but not quite wet.

Serves 4

2–3 large fennel bulbs, fronds reserved and finely chopped

120ml (4fl oz) extra virgin olive oil

6 garlic cloves: 5 finely chopped, 1 left whole

2 tsp fennel seeds

60g (2¼oz) pitted green olives, roughly chopped

100g (3½oz) breadcrumbs

½ tsp red chilli flakes (optional)

400g (14oz) orecchiette

flaky sea salt

Cut each fennel bulb into 8 wedges. Add the fennel to a large pan of salted, simmering water and boil for 2 minutes. Drain and return the fennel to the pan, adding half the olive oil, the chopped garlic, fennel seeds and a good pinch of salt. Stir well and put the lid on. Turn the heat to very low and cook for 10–20 minutes, stirring and scraping from time to time; the fennel should become completely tender. Stir in the olives.

Meanwhile, make the pangrattato. Heat the rest of the olive oil in a heavy-based pan over a medium heat. Add the whole garlic clove and the breadcrumbs and stir well. Cook, stirring constantly, until the crumbs turn golden and crisp. Using a slotted spoon, remove the breadcrumbs to a plate lined with kitchen paper and discard the garlic clove.

Add the fennel fronds to the garlicky fennel and check the seasoning, adding salt and chilli flakes (if using) to taste.

Bring a large pan of salted water to the boil and cook the orecchiette until just retaining a little bite. Drain, reserving a cup of the pasta water. Stir the pasta into the fennel, adding just enough pasta water to get the right consistency.

Serve topped with the pangrattato.

VEGAN: Yes.
GF: Use GF pasta and breadcrumbs.
SEASONAL SWAPS: This is as adaptable as it gets – try it with skinned chopped tomatoes, steamed asparagus or shredded fried sprouts, for a start.

CELERIAC + SHALLOT PAPPARDELLE

The secret to the pleasure here is the combination of sweet earthiness from the celeriac, sweetness and a hint of bitterness from the burnt shallots, the faintest hint of bitterness behind parsley's fresh flavour and the warm contrast from the gremolata and nutmeg.

Of course, feel free to switch to whichever flat pasta you prefer, and if you have the oven on for something else anytime in the couple of days before you make this, you can roast the shallots ahead. This can handle a little Parmesan but sometimes I prefer pasta without and that's usually the case here.

Serves 4

300g (10oz) celeriac, peeled and chopped into 3cm (1¼in) pieces

250ml (9fl oz) milk

a grating of nutmeg

4 large shallots, unpeeled

40g (1½oz) walnuts, lightly toasted

small bunch of flat-leaf parsley

1 garlic clove, peeled

finely grated zest of 1 orange

400g (14oz) pappardelle

extra virgin olive oil, for drizzling (optional)

flaky sea salt and freshly ground black pepper

Put the celeriac into a medium-sized pan with the milk, nutmeg and a good pinch of salt. Simmer for 15–20 minutes, or until the celeriac is tender.

Preheat the grill (broiler) to high and cook the shallots under the grill – not too close – until softened and blackened, turning often. Once cool enough, squeeze out of their skins and roughly chop on a board.

Prepare the gremolata by finely chopping the walnuts, parsley and garlic and combining with the orange zest.

Transfer the celeriac to a blender and whizz until smooth, using a little bit of the cooking liquid if needed; taste and add a little salt, pepper and nutmeg if needed. Stir in the shallots and either keep warm or keep to one side to reheat.

Cook the pappardelle in plenty of salted water at a rolling boil until al dente – offering a little resistance to the bite. Drain, reserving a cupful of the pasta water. Add the pasta to the celeriac/shallot sauce, adding a few tablespoons of the pasta water to loosen if needed.

Serve topped with the gremolata. Dash with a little olive oil if you fancy.

VEGAN: Use plant-based milk.
GF: Use GF pasta.
SEASONAL SWAPS: Jerusalem artichokes and parsnips are great substitutions for the celeriac.

TOMATO, BEAN + OLIVE LINGUINI

Tomatoes and green beans are one of my favourite summer combinations, and floral marjoram (oregano, if you prefer) and the salty punch of the olives just makes it sing even better. The recipe uses canned tomatoes so that you are free to make it whenever, but if you have half a kilo of fresh tomatoes, skin them – a couple of minutes submerged in boiling water should have their skins slipping off easily – and chop, before adding when you'd add the canned.

I've made this with pangrattato (breadcrumbs fried with oil and garlic – page 100) and very fine it is too, but the almonds might just win in this case: choose whichever makes you happy.

Serves 4

5 tbsp extra virgin olive oil, plus more to finish

3 garlic cloves: 2 thinly sliced, 1 left whole

4 tbsp flaked almonds

400g (14oz) green beans, trimmed

1 tbsp red wine vinegar

400g (14oz) can chopped tomatoes

large pinch of dried chilli flakes

50g (2oz) pitted black olives

large bunch of fresh marjoram or oregano

500g (1lb 2oz) long pasta such as linguine or spaghetti

flaky sea salt and freshly ground black pepper

Heat 1 tablespoon of the olive oil in a sauté pan over a medium heat, add the whole garlic clove and cook for 1 minute until aromatic. Add the almonds and a pinch of salt and cook for a couple of minutes until golden, stirring often. Tip onto a sheet of kitchen paper, discarding the garlic.

Heat 3 tablespoons of the olive oil in the same pan over a medium heat, add the beans and sliced garlic with a pinch of salt and cook for a couple of minutes.

Add the vinegar, tomatoes, chilli flakes and about 200ml (7fl oz) boiling water. Cover the pan with a lid, turn the heat down to low and cook for 25–30 minutes until the beans have completely softened. You may need to add a splash more water from time to time.

Stir in the olives and herbs and add the remaining tablespoon of olive oil, then season with salt and pepper if needed.

Cook the pasta in a large pan of boiling water according to the packet instructions, then drain (reserving a little of the water) and stir into the beans, adding a touch of the pasta cooking liquid if needed.

Serve scattered with the almonds.

VEGAN: Yes.
GF: Use GF pasta.
SEASONAL SWAPS: This is really all about the partnership of tomatoes and beans, but do try this with asparagus in spring.

PASTA SHELLS
+ SPRING RAGU

Surely, 100g of large pasta shells – maybe a dozen pieces – is nowhere near as much as the same weight of small pasta shapes? Three bites and the former is gone. And so, my greedy mind compels me to make too much large shell pasta almost every time. Still, as a floppy scoop for sauces there is much to commend it, and this shows its abilities off beautifully. These mini-conches hold so much flavour within.

I love salted ricotta's soft sourness, but it works differently well with feta or Parmesan.

Serves 4

400g (14oz) large shell pasta, such as conchiglioni

3 tbsp extra virgin olive oil, plus more to serve

bunch of spring onions (scallions), sliced

3 garlic cloves, finely chopped

300g (10oz) peas (fresh or frozen)

300g (10oz) podded smallish broad (fava) beans, boiled for about 1 minute until tender, then drained

300ml (10fl oz) vegetable stock (page 192, or use good shop-bought)

100g (3½oz) spinach or chard leaves, washed and cut into broad ribbons

small bunch of chopped herbs (basil, mint or oregano)

60g (2¼oz) salted ricotta, crumbled or coarsely grated (or use Parmesan or feta)

flaky sea salt and freshly ground black pepper

Bring a large pan of salted water to the boil and cook the pasta according to the packet instructions, or until al dente.

Meanwhile, heat the oil in a heavy-based saucepan over a medium heat, add the spring onions and cook for about 2 minutes to soften. Add the garlic and cook for 1 minute more, then stir in the peas and beans. Stir well and cook for 2 minutes.

Add the hot stock and a big pinch of salt and simmer for about 10 minutes until all the vegetables are very tender but not mushy. Add the spinach or chard and cook for a further 2 minutes until completely wilted. Remove from the heat and stir in the herbs and half the cheese. Check the seasoning, adding pepper and more salt if needed.

Add the pasta shells to the ragu and toss gently to combine, before spooning into bowls. Drizzle each bowlful of pasta with a little extra olive oil and crumble over the rest of the cheese.

VEGAN: Use plant-based cheese.
GF: Use GF pasta.
SEASONAL SWAPS: A late summer version using runner beans and chard for the broad beans and spinach is delightful.

ASPARAGUS, PEA + SHALLOT FETTUCCINE

Saffron reminds me in scent and flavour of a leaky Bic biro, and its delightful bitterness contrasts and perfectly enhances the sweetness of the asparagus, peas and shallots here. If you are using fresh peas, throw a handful of the pods into the water to enhance the flavour as the pasta cooks.

Serves 4

50g (2oz) unsalted butter

3 shallots, finely chopped

a generous pinch of saffron

2 garlic cloves, finely chopped

15ml (5fl oz) double (heavy) cream

small bunch of flat-leaf parsley or chives, finely chopped

400g (14oz) fettuccine, or another flat egg pasta noodle

bunch of asparagus, trimmed and thinly sliced

300g (10oz) peas (fresh or frozen)

flaky sea salt and freshly ground black pepper

shaved Parmesan, to serve

Melt the butter in a heavy-based pan over a medium heat, add the shallots and cook for 5–7 minutes until soft but without any colour. Add the saffron and garlic and cook for a minute before adding the cream and cooking for 2 minutes to thicken. Season with salt and pepper and stir in the herbs.

Meanwhile cook the fettuccine until al dente according to the packet instructions, adding the asparagus and peas for the last 2 minutes.

Drain the pasta and vegetables thoroughly, reserving some of the water, and stir into the saffron cream. If the sauce is too thick, add a few tablespoons of the pasta cooking water to loosen the mix.

Serve with plenty of shaved Parmesan at the table.

VEGAN: Use plant-based cream, butter and cheese.
GF: Use GF pasta.
SEASONAL SWAPS: Sprouting broccoli or calabrese are excellent cold weather variations, should you fancy this in winter.

Pies a

nd tarts

CRÈME FRAÎCHE
+ TOMATO TART

This is a tweak on a tart recipe in my book *Sour*, with the watercress adding brightness and a little extra nose-tingling to go with the mustard. The sweetness of the tomato's flesh works so well against the sourness of its juice, the crème fraîche and the vinegar in the mustard – and the watercress kicks it all along beautifully. It is seriously good. The pastry is shorter than a Mod's fringe, which is exactly as it should be.

Serves 4

For the pastry
250g (9oz) plain (all-purpose) flour, plus extra for dusting
pinch of salt
150g (5oz) butter
1 medium egg, beaten

For the filling
400g (14oz) medium or small tomatoes, cut in half
4 tbsp extra virgin olive oil
300g (10oz) crème fraîche
2 garlic cloves, finely chopped
1 tbsp Dijon mustard
4–5 sprigs of watercress, thicker stalks removed
flaky sea salt and freshly ground black pepper

Preheat the oven to 190°C/170°C fan/375°F.

Put the flour, salt and butter into a food processor and pulse until the mixture resembles fine breadcrumbs. Add the egg and pulse again until it just comes together. Bring the dough together with your hands and shape into a flat round. Wrap in clingfilm (plastic wrap) and chill in the fridge for 30 minutes.

Lay the tomatoes on a tray lined with baking parchment and drizzle with half the olive oil and some salt and pepper. Roast in the oven for 6–8 minutes until softened but still retaining their shape. Allow to cool.

Lightly butter a 20cm (8in) springform tart tin. Remove the pastry from the fridge, flatten it with a rolling pin and then, using your fingers and the heel of your hand, evenly push the pastry out over the surface of the tin, pushing it up the sides and into the corners of the tin.

Beat together the crème fraîche, garlic, mustard, a pinch of salt and a generous twist of black pepper. Add any juices from the tomato roasting tray and spread the mixture over the tart case. Arrange the tomatoes over the top.

Place in the centre of the oven and bake for 20–25 minutes until the pastry is crisp and the tomatoes are golden.

Leave the tart to cool for 5 minutes before turning out. Scatter it with the watercress, drizzled with the remaining olive oil, and serve in wedges, either warm or at room temperature.

VEGAN: Use plant-based crème fraîche and shop-bought vegan pastry.
GF: Use GF flour or shop-bought GF pastry.
SEASONAL SWAPS: This is nicely adaptable, as long as the vegetable in place of the tomatoes is similarly soft and the leaves have a kick – roasted carrot in place of tomato, and rocket (arugula) in place of watercress are great alternatives.

ARTICHOKE + SPRING ONION PIE

This delight is a very close relation of the Greek filo pie spanakopita (if you like that you'll love this) but spanakopita means 'spinach and cheese pie', and you'll notice the absence of spinach in this dish. Cooked globe artichokes – sweet, with a hint of bitter grassiness – are perfect here, and yes, you could cook your own, but a jar of ready-cooked makes life easy when time is tight. As good as this is a few minutes after coming out of the oven, it might just be at its best cold for lunch the day after. It is most certainly perfect picnic food.

Serves 4

1 onion, finely chopped

150g (5oz) melted butter

bunch of spring onions (scallions), very thinly sliced

2 garlic cloves, thinly sliced

500g (1lb 2oz) artichoke hearts in oil, drained

40g (1½oz) coarse bulgur, rinsed and drained

200g (7oz) crumbled feta cheese

200g (7oz) ricotta

4 eggs, beaten

large bunch of fennel or dill fronds, finely chopped

small bunch of flat-leaf parsley, finely chopped

10 sheets of filo (phyllo) pastry

1 tsp fennel seeds

flaky sea salt and freshly ground black pepper

In a medium pan, fry the onion in 1 tablespoon of the melted butter for 10 minutes, stirring occasionally, until soft. Add the spring onions and garlic and cook for 1–2 minutes, then remove from the heat.

Preheat the oven to 190°C/170°C fan/375°F.

In a large bowl, combine the artichokes, the cooked onion mixture, bulgur, feta, ricotta, eggs, herbs and a good pinch of salt and plenty of pepper.

Lay two filo sheets vertically in a baking dish, about 30 x 20cm (12 x 8in) or 25cm (10in) in diameter. Brush each sheet with melted butter. Take two more filo sheets and lay at 90 degrees, brushing each sheet you add with melted butter. Continue to arrange filo sheets in a clockwork fashion, incrementally overlapping them and brushing each filo sheet with butter as you go.

Place the artichoke mixture in the centre and fold the filo sheets over the mixture, then brush with the remaining butter and sprinkle with the fennel seeds.

Bake for 25–30 minutes until golden and the centre is just set. Remove from the oven and leave to cool for 5–10 minutes before slicing and serving.

VEGAN: No, but if you want to make it dairy-free, use plant-based feta and ricotta, or similar; an equal mix of plant-based butter with olive oil (from the jarred artichokes) works better here than just swapping butter for plant-based butter.
GF: Use GF filo pastry and use quinoa instead of bulgur wheat.
SEASONAL SWAPS: Diced, roasted vegetables – celeriac, Jerusalem artichokes, carrots – or roasted summer vegetables – (bell) peppers, tomatoes and aubergines (eggplants) – work so well instead of the artichokes.

PEPPER, TOMATO + OLIVE GALETTE

This is as informal a coming together of pastry and topping as it gets. If you are apprehensive, make this with shop-bought puff pastry and, once confident, move on to the pastry below. With this under your belt, you can then play with the toppings: treat it with the creativity you would a pizza.

Serves 4

For the pastry (or use 1 sheet of shop-bought ready-rolled puff or shortcrust pastry)

200g (7oz) plain (all-purpose) flour, plus extra for dusting

½ tsp salt

100g (3 ½ oz) chilled butter, diced

60ml (4 tbsp) ice-cold water

1 egg, beaten

1 tbsp milk

For the filling

2 tbsp extra virgin olive oil

1 onion, thinly sliced

1 red (bell) pepper, thinly sliced

1 yellow (bell) pepper, thinly sliced

1 tbsp white wine vinegar

2 garlic cloves, thinly sliced

80g (3oz) pitted black olives, roughly chopped

400g (14oz) cherry tomatoes, halved

a few generous sprigs of thyme

flaky sea salt and freshly ground black pepper

If making your own pastry, put the flour, salt and butter into a food processor and pulse until the mixture resembles fine breadcrumbs. Mix in the cold water and stir with a blunt knife until it comes together. Turn out onto a lightly floured surface and gently knead the dough a few times – don't overwork it – until it forms a rough ball. Roll out into a rectangle, about 1cm (½in) thick.

Fold the bottom third of the rectangle into the centre, then fold the top third over the top and rotate 90 degrees. Repeat the rolling and folding process two more times, for a total of three folds. Wrap the pastry in a bag or baking parchment and chill in the fridge for at least 30 minutes.

Preheat the oven to 200°C/180°C fan/400°F.

Heat the oil in a medium pan over a medium heat, add the onion and peppers and cook in the oil for 10 minutes or so until soft. Stir in the vinegar and garlic and cook for 1 minute. Remove from the heat.

On a lightly floured surface, roll out the dough into a rectangle about 40 x 25cm (16 x 10in). Alternatively, unroll the shop-bought pastry sheet. Place on a baking sheet lined with baking parchment.

Spread the pepper mix over the dough, leaving a small border around the edges. Scatter the olives over the peppers, followed by the cherry tomatoes, and season with salt and pepper.

In a cup, combine the beaten egg and milk to make an egg wash, then use this to brush the edges of the dough. Bake in the centre of the oven for 25–30 minutes until the crust is golden and the filling is bubbling. Remove from the oven and allow to cool for a few minutes before serving, sprinkled with thyme leaves.

VEGAN: Use plant-based cream and shop-bought vegan pastry.

GF: Use GF flour or shop-bought gluten-free pastry.

SEASONAL SWAPS: This is nicely adaptable to any season: thinly sliced fennel and courgette (zucchini) for summer, roasted carrots, parsnips and shallots in autumn, Jerusalem artichokes and leeks in winter, and spring onions (scallions) and asparagus in spring.

SPRING ONION + TARRAGON TART

If you have pastry anxiety that deprives you of the pleasure of a pie or tart, try this: it is as simple and delicious as it gets. And if you are nervous about making tarts in general, or are feeling idle, do as I often do and use 400g (14oz) shortcrust pastry from the shop.

Serves 4

For the pastry

250g (9oz) plain (all-purpose) flour, plus extra for dusting

1 tsp salt

125g (4oz) chilled butter, cubed

3 tbsp ice-cold water

For the filling

3 bunches of spring onions (scallions), trimmed and halved lengthways

2 tbsp white wine vinegar

4 eggs, beaten

400ml (14fl oz) double (heavy) cream

leaves from 5 sprigs of tarragon, finely chopped

flaky sea salt and freshly ground black pepper

Put the flour, salt and butter into a food processor and pulse until the mixture resembles fine breadcrumbs. Alternatively, in a bowl using your fingertips, mix the butter into the flour and salt until it resembles breadcrumbs. Sprinkle over the water and bring the dough together with your hands until there are no dry crumbs left. Flatten into a rough circle, wrap well, then chill for about 30 minutes.

Preheat the oven to 180°C/160°C fan/350°F.

Lightly flour the work surface, then roll out the pastry to fit a tart tin about 20cm (8in) in diameter. The pastry should be around 4mm (¼in) thick. Leave the edges of the pastry bigger than the tin, as it will shrink a little during cooking. Prick the base of the pastry with a fork and line with baking parchment. Fill with baking beans (pie weights) and blind bake for 20 minutes.

While the case is cooking, put the spring onions and vinegar into a roasting tray with some salt and pepper and roast for 7–10 minutes until softened.

Remove the parchment and beans from the case, brush the pastry with a little of the beaten egg and then return to the oven for 10 minutes until the pastry is golden. Carefully trim the edges of the pastry with a sharp knife, then turn the oven down to 170°C/150°C fan/340°F.

Mix the eggs and the cream together, season with salt and pepper and add half the chopped tarragon leaves. Pour the filling into the pastry case and add three-quarters of the spring onions, the rest of the tarragon and a little black pepper evenly across the tart. Bake in the oven for 20–25 minutes until the filling is set.

Leave the tart to cool completely before removing from the tin. Serve topped with the remaining spring onions.

VEGAN: No – try as I might, I have not found a satisfactory way of substituting the eggs in this.

GF: Use GF plain flour or shop-bought GF pastry.

SEASONAL SWAPS: Try this with just-blanched asparagus, tenderstem broccoli, leeks and so on.

SHALLOT + BEETROOT TARTE TATIN

I do love the glorious marriage of sweet-sour vegetables with crisp puff pastry that is a tarte Tatin, but there is always an element of jeopardy; in the inversion of tart to plate lies so much of the success. The secret is paying attention so as not to overcook the caramel, and to invert the tart carefully (nobody needs a caramel tattoo on their forearm) but swiftly.

A salad of green leaves, dressed in a lively, sharp dressing is the ideal accompaniment.

Serves 4

8 small beetroots (beet)

50g (2oz) caster (superfine) sugar

40g (1½oz) butter, plus extra to grease

2 tbsp red wine vinegar

2 tsp thyme leaves

8 small shallots, peeled but left whole

375g (13oz) sheet of ready-rolled puff pastry

flaky sea salt and freshly ground black pepper

Preheat the oven to 200°C/180°C fan/400°F.

Wrap the beetroots in a double layer of foil and roast for 20 minutes until tender. Allow to cool until they are cool enough to peel, then cut in half.

Put the sugar in a large, heavy-based frying pan or skillet. Heat very gently until the sugar dissolves and turns golden. Add the butter and vinegar, then stir with a wooden spoon to combine. Add half the thyme, the shallots and beetroot halves, cut-side down, and cook for about 5 minutes, seasoning with salt and pepper.

Cut a round of pastry slightly larger than the frying pan or skillet, place it on top of the vegetables and tuck the edges down the sides. Place in the centre of the oven and bake for 20–25 minutes until the pastry is puffed up and golden. Remove from the oven and allow to rest for 5 minutes, before carefully – but swiftly – inverting onto a plate.

Scatter with the rest of the thyme leaves and more black pepper.

VEGAN: Use plant-based butter and ensure the pastry is vegan.
GF: Use GF puff pastry.
SEASONAL SWAPS: The tarte Tatin treatment suits many vegetables; a combination of summer vegetables such as tomatoes, baby onions and peppers, or a selection of diced root vegetables, are well worth your time.

MUSHROOM + VEGETABLE PIE

If you aren't familiar with Jeremy Lee, allow me to encourage you towards his Quo Vadis restaurant in London's Soho. Of the many things that will delight, he always has a pie on the menu, and whatever form that pie takes it is exceptional. I thought of him the other day while eating this, momentarily hopeful that he might appreciate it in all its seasonal simplicity.

Serves 4

For the pastry

150g (5oz) wholemeal or spelt flour, plus extra for dusting (or use plain/all-purpose)

150g (5oz) self-raising flour

1 tsp salt

150g (5oz) chilled butter, diced

1 egg, beaten

For the filling

800g (1lb 12oz) mixed root vegetables, cut into 2cm (¾in) dice

3 celery sticks, chopped

4 tsp extra virgin olive oil

60g (2¼oz) butter

1 onion, finely chopped

40g (1½oz) plain (all-purpose) flour

600ml (1¼ pints) milk, heated

400g mushrooms, finely chopped

½ small bunch of tarragon, finely chopped

flaky sea salt and freshly ground black pepper

Preheat the oven to 200°C/180°C fan/400°F.

Toss the root vegetables, celery and olive oil into a roasting tray and season generously with salt and pepper. Roast in the oven for 25–30 minutes until just taking the point of a knife and holding their shape.

Meanwhile, to make the pastry, tip the flours and salt into a bowl, add the butter and rub it into the flour with your fingers, until you have a breadcrumb texture with the odd lump of butter. Add 3 tablespoons ice-cold water and use a knife to stir until it starts to clump, then bring together with your hands – depending on the flour, you may need a tablespoon more water. Wrap and chill in the fridge for 30 minutes.

For the filling, melt 40g (1½oz) of the butter in a large pan over a medium heat and add the onion and a big pinch of salt. Cook for 5–10 minutes until softened, then stir in the flour and cook for 1 minute. Add the milk a little at a time, whisking well until combined. Cook, stirring every now and then, until thick and creamy.

Add the rest of the butter to a frying pan and cook the mushrooms over a medium heat until they release their liquid and it cooks away. Add to the sauce, along with the tarragon and roasted vegetables, and season to taste with salt and pepper.

Lightly flour the work surface and roll out two-thirds of the pastry until about 3mm thick. Line a deep 20cm (8in) pie tin, leaving a few centimetres overhanging. Chill in the fridge while you roll out the rest of the pastry as a lid.

Spoon the filling into the pie dish, then top with the pastry lid, trimming the overhang. Crimp the edges with a finger or fork to seal. Brush with the beaten egg, then bake for 40 minutes until golden. Leave to rest for 10 minutes before serving.

VEGAN: Use oat milk and plant-based butter. Use shop-bought vegan pastry – brush with oak milk instead of egg.
GF: Use shop-bought GF pastry and GF plain flour.
SEASONAL SWAPS: I like to keep carrot the consistent element, with the rest made up of any of celeriac, swede, parsnip, turnips, potato or Jerusalem artichokes. By all means, add leafy greens, and/or substitute the celery for chard. Tarragon is made for mushrooms, but thyme, rosemary and sage are superb options too.

GARDENER'S PIE

Do the three early steps at the same time or one after the other, depending on your confidence. This is a Gardener's Pie – no shepherds (nor their flock) have been involved here – as I wanted to draw your attention to just how good and savoury the classic lamb dish can be without meat. I prefer it. The miso brings the savoury satisfaction that sits underneath the vegetables and lentils, but the slow build-up of vegetable flavour is what creates complexity. Serve this with green vegetables – sprouts, kale or a good deeply coloured cabbage are particular favourites.

Serves 4

4 tbsp extra virgin olive oil

3 celery sticks, finely chopped

1 onion, finely chopped

2 carrots, finely chopped

1 leek, finely chopped

300g (10oz) mushrooms, finely chopped

500g (1lb 2oz) potatoes, peeled and diced

500g (1lb 2oz) swede, peeled and diced

freshly grated nutmeg

100ml (3½fl oz) milk

2 tbsp red miso

2 tbsp finely chopped sage, rosemary or thyme leaves

2 tbsp tomato purée (paste)

200g (7oz) chopped tomatoes (canned is fine)

2 garlic cloves, finely chopped

40g (1½oz) Puy (French) lentils, soaked in cold water for 30–60 minutes, then drained

400ml (14fl oz) vegetable stock (page 192, or use good shop-bought)

flaky sea salt and freshly ground black pepper

Heat 2 tablespoons of the oil in a medium pan over a medium heat; when it runs thin, add the celery, onion, carrots and leek along with a generous pinch of salt, and – lowering the heat a touch – cook for 15 minutes or so until soft and glossy, stirring often. Add the mushrooms and cook for a further 5 minutes or so.

In a large pan of salted water, boil the potatoes and swede until tender. Drain and return the potatoes and swede to the pan, then use a fork to mash them together, seasoning with salt, pepper and an enthusiastic scratch of nutmeg. Stir in the milk, 1 tablespoon of the miso and the remaining 2 tablespoons of olive oil.

Stir the herbs, tomato purée, tomatoes, garlic and the remaining tablespoon of miso into the celery mix and cook for 5 minutes over a medium heat. Stir in the lentils and stock and simmer for 30 minutes until the lentils are tender and the sauce is rich and thick.

Preheat the oven to 180°C/160°C fan/350°F.

Spoon the lentil mixture into an ovenproof dish and spread or pipe the potato mixture on top. Bake for 30–40 minutes until piping hot, finishing off under the grill (broiler) to brown the top if it needs it.

VEGAN: Use plant-based milk.
GF: Yes.
SEASONAL SWAPS: Vary the mashed vegetable topping as you wish, while retaining the overall quantity – celeriac, Jerusalem artichoke and turnip are so good; and switch to other lentils (red are differently good here) if you fancy too.

CAULIFLOWER, POTATO + CARAWAY HOMITY PIE

Even in the small towns of south-west England in the late 1980s, the occasional health-food shop and wholefood cafe could be found, an island of nutrition in a sea of Spacedust and limeade. Their menus invariably featured at least one thing from the genuinely game-changing *Cranks Recipe Book*. Very often that was homity pie, a carb-heavy coming-together of potatoes, cream, cheese and pastry. Even writing those words makes me simultaneously ravenous and keen to listen to 'Sign of the Times'. Here is a gorgeous variation on its theme.

Serves 4

For the pastry

250g (9oz) plain (all-purpose) flour, plus extra for dusting

pinch of salt

1 tsp caraway seeds, lightly cracked in a mortar and pestle

150g (5oz) butter

1 egg, beaten, plus extra for brushing

For the filling

500g (1lb 2oz) new potatoes, peeled and thinly sliced (about 1cm/½in thick)

30g (1oz) butter or extra virgin olive oil

1 large onion, thinly sliced

½ smallish cauliflower, thinly sliced

150g (5oz) Cheddar, coarsely grated or crumbled small

¼ freshly grated whole nutmeg

small bunch of chives, thinly sliced

250ml (9fl oz) double (heavy) cream

flaky sea salt and freshly ground black pepper

Put the flour, salt, caraway seeds and butter into a food processor and blend until the mixture resembles fine breadcrumbs. Add the egg and pulse until the mixture just comes together. Alternatively, using your fingertips, rub the butter into the flour and salt until it resembles breadcrumbs. Add the egg and mix to form a dough. Bring the dough together with your hands and shape into a round. Wrap in clingfilm (plastic wrap) and chill in the fridge for 30 minutes while you make the filling.

Cook the potatoes in boiling salted water until just tender, about 15 minutes. Drain well and allow to dry.

Melt the butter in a large pan over a medium heat and fry the onion for about 8–10 minutes until soft. Stir in the cauliflower, cover and cook for 5–10 minutes, stirring often until the cauliflower begins to soften. Add the potatoes and half the cheese. Season the mix with the nutmeg, chives and some salt and pepper.

Meanwhile, preheat the oven to 180°C/160°C fan/350°F.

Lightly flour the work surface, then roll out the pastry to fit a tart tin about 20cm (8in) in diameter. The pastry should be around 4mm (¼in) thick. Leave the edges of the pastry bigger than the tin, as it will shrink a little during cooking. Prick the base of the pastry with a fork and line with baking parchment. Fill with baking beans (pie weights) and blind bake for 20 minutes.

Remove the parchment and beans from the case, brush the pastry with a little beaten egg and return to the oven for 10 minutes until the pastry is golden. Trim the edges of the pastry with a sharp knife, then turn the oven down to 170°C/150°C fan/340°F.

Spoon the filling mixture evenly into the tart case and pour over the cream. Sprinkle with the remaining cheese and bake in the hot oven for 35–40 minutes until the pastry is crisp and the filling is set and lightly golden. Leave to cool in the tin for 5 minutes or so before cutting into wedges. Serve warm or at room temperature.

VEGAN: Use shop-bought pastry (most brands are vegan) and sprinkle the caraway over it before blind baking; use plant-based cheese, butter and cream.
GF: Use GF flour or shop-bought gluten-free pastry sprinkled with caraway seeds.
SEASONAL SWAPS: Try Broccoli and Romanesco in place of the cauliflower.

Son

nething
baked

CREAMY CHICORY GRATIN

This gratin has a wonderful balance of sharp, aromatic and chilli heat, but what really makes it is the way the gentle bitterness of chicory relaxes perfectly into its sofa of dairy. I've used Urfa chilli flakes (often sold as Urfa pepper) as they are mild, raisiny and smoky, which suits this beautifully; by all means use another if you prefer.

I suggest you leave the room and ideally the house while this is cooking: the scent of comfort will leak from the oven and turn any inklings of hunger into a raging appetite.

Serves 4

2 bay leaves

1 tbsp white wine vinegar

4 large pointed heads of chicory (endive), halved lengthways

30g (1oz) butter, plus more for greasing

30g (1oz) plain (all-purpose) flour

300ml (10fl oz) milk

1 tsp thyme leaves

2 tbsp Dijon mustard

freshly grated nutmeg

100g (3½oz) grated Gruyère (aged is best)

½–1 tsp Urfa chilli flakes

flaky sea salt and freshly ground black pepper

Preheat the oven to 200°C/180°C fan/400°F and lightly butter a gratin dish.

Bring a pan of salted water to the boil with the bay leaves and the vinegar. Add the chicory and simmer for 3–4 minutes. Drain, discarding the bay leaves and keeping about 200ml (7fl oz) of the cooking liquid. Arrange the chicory halves in the gratin dish cut-side up.

Meanwhile, in a small pan, cook the butter and flour together over a medium heat for a couple of minutes until it bubbles, then – bit by bit – whisk in the milk until fully incorporated, followed by the reserved cooking liquid. Cook for 5 minutes until smooth and thick, stirring often. Add the thyme, mustard and a good grating of nutmeg and season generously with salt and pepper, stirring well.

Pour the sauce over the chicory and press down so it oozes through. Top with the grated cheese and bake in the oven until golden, about 20 minutes. Allow to rest for a few minutes before sprinkling with chilli flakes and serving with a green salad.

VEGAN: Use plant-based butter, milk and cheese.
GF: Use GF plain flour.
SEASONAL SWAPS: Asparagus, broccolis of all kinds, cauliflower and even little gems are among the many vegetables that are happy in place of the chicory.

TOMATOES STUFFED WITH SPICED COCONUT RICE

As I've written numerous times, a marrow is a torpedo of compost with no more business on a dinner plate than my old man's hanky. Every autumn, recipes appear for stuffed marrow, seemingly on the basis that filling a canoe with spiced loveliness somehow makes the canoe worth eating. This is the antidote to those with a phobia of stuffed vegetables caused by marrows. Serve this with a green bean salad, a selection of lettuce leaves, and/or the potato and egg salad on page 42.

Serves 4

8–12 medium tomatoes
150g (5oz) basmati rice
2 tbsp coconut oil
1 small onion, finely chopped
3 garlic cloves, thinly sliced
2 tbsp finely grated
fresh ginger
1 tsp ground cumin
1 tsp ground coriander
½ tsp ground turmeric
½ tsp chilli powder
200ml (7fl oz) vegetable
stock (page 192, or use
good shop-bought)
100ml (3½fl oz) coconut
cream or coconut milk
flaky sea salt and freshly
ground black pepper

For the tarka
2 tbsp coconut oil
1 tsp cumin seeds
1 tsp mustard seeds
1 green chilli, thinly sliced
20 fresh curry leaves
(or use dried)

Preheat the oven to 200°C/180°C fan/400°F.

Cut the tops off the tomatoes and set the tops aside for later. Use a teaspoon to scoop out and discard the seeds and pulp.

Rinse the basmati rice under cold water until the water runs clear, then drain.

Warm the coconut oil in a medium pan, add the onion and cook for 10 minutes or so, stirring occasionally, until softened and translucent. Add half the garlic, the ginger, cumin, coriander, turmeric and chilli powder to the onions. Cook for a minute until fragrant, then stir in the vegetable stock and bring to the boil.

Reduce the heat to low, add the rice and stir, then cover the pan with a lid and let the rice simmer for about 12–15 minutes until the rice is cooked and the liquid absorbed. Stir in the coconut cream or milk. Taste and season if necessary.

Fill each hollowed tomato with the spiced rice and place a tomato lid on each. Place the stuffed tomatoes in a lightly oiled baking dish and bake for 20–25 minutes until the tomatoes are softened and slightly roasted.

While they are cooking, heat the coconut oil over a medium heat in a small pan. Add the cumin seeds, mustard seeds, the remaining garlic, the sliced chilli and curry leaves and cook for 1–2 minutes until the seeds are popping. Remove from the heat.

Drizzle the crisp curry leaf tarka over the stuffed tomatoes and serve.

VEGAN: Yes.
GF: Yes.
SEASONAL SWAPS: This works brilliantly with halved aubergines (eggplants), (bell) peppers or medium courgettes (zucchini). You are forbidden to use marrows.

SPROUTING BROCCOLI + LEEK GRATIN

This simple, delicious delight is welcome on all but the hottest days of high summer. It's also highly adaptable – a real family favourite that's quick, nutritious and satisfying.

While you can cook this in a deeper dish, a wide, shallow dish gives just the right mix of creaminess to crunch ratio. Serve with a high pile of leaves dressed just with olive oil.

Serves 4

2 garlic cloves, finely chopped

1 tbsp finely chopped fresh rosemary

250ml (9fl oz) double (heavy) cream

500g (1lb 2oz) leeks, trimmed and sliced into 3–4cm (1¼–1½in) pieces

3 tbsp extra virgin olive oil

500g (1lb 2oz) sprouting broccoli, thick stalks trimmed

50g (2oz) hazelnuts, finely chopped

35g (1¼oz) Parmesan, finely grated

flaky sea salt and freshly ground black pepper

Preheat the oven to 200°C/180°C fan/400°F.

In a bowl, stir the garlic, rosemary and a good tweak of salt and pepper into the cream. Place the leeks in a single layer in a baking dish, drizzle with the olive oil, season with salt and pepper and roast for 15–20 minutes until cooked through and beginning to colour in places.

Add the sprouting broccoli to a pan of boiling salted water and cook for just 1 minute. Drain well. Arrange the cooked broccoli on top of the leeks, pour over the seasoned cream and scatter evenly with the hazelnuts and Parmesan. Season with a little salt and pepper. Bake in the oven for 15–20 minutes until bubbling and golden in places.

VEGAN: Use plant-based cream and cheese.
GF: Yes.
SEASONAL SWAPS: Tenderstem broccoli, halved sprouts, asparagus, halved pak choi (bok choy) and cauliflower all swap in for the sprouting broccoli, while onions and shallots can substitute for the leeks.

AUBERGINES, TOMATOES, POLENTA + SPICED CREAM

I almost always eat this on a Monday evening, having made the polenta while arsing about in the kitchen on the Sunday. Not that it's the biggest chore, but cook it ahead and this is the least troublesome supper on a work night, when the prospect of even a moment of whisking might feel too much.

I used to make this with the rosemary added before cooking but the nature of the dish means little flavour penetrates or remains – the rosemary leaves scorch to bitterness, losing their oily pungency to the heat of the oven – so I sprinkle finely chopped leaves on at the end and it works beautifully.

Serves 4

4 aubergines (eggplants)

800ml (1¼ pints) vegetable stock (page 192, or use good shop-bought) or water

125g (4½oz) coarse ground polenta

30g (1oz) butter, plus more for greasing

20g (¾oz) Parmesan, finely grated

300g (10oz) cherry tomatoes

3 garlic cloves, finely chopped

½ tsp paprika

big pinch of saffron

250ml (9fl oz) double (heavy) cream

1 tbsp fresh rosemary, finely chopped

flaky sea salt and freshly ground black pepper

Cut the aubergines in half lengthways and score the cut sides in a diamond pattern. Sprinkle with salt and leave cut-side down in a colander.

In a large pan, bring the stock to a simmer. Pour in the polenta in a thin stream, whisking constantly to prevent lumps. Once incorporated, use a wooden spoon to stir constantly for 5 minutes as it cooks. Turn the heat down low and continue to cook gently for 15–20 minutes, giving it a vigorous stir every couple of minutes. Stir in half the butter and the Parmesan, then remove from the heat, season with salt and plenty of pepper and pour into a lightly buttered tray. Allow to cool before cutting into cubes.

Preheat the oven to 200°C/180°C fan/400°F.

Use kitchen paper or a tea towel to dry the aubergines, place on a lightly greased roasting tray cut-side up and cook in the oven for 5 minutes until slightly softened.

Add the polenta cubes and cherry tomatoes to the tray, dotted around the aubergine, and return to the oven for 15–20 minutes until the polenta is lightly browned and crisp and the aubergines and cherry tomatoes are cooked.

In a small frying pan over a medium heat, cook the garlic in the remaining butter for 1 minute, then add the paprika and saffron and cook for a few seconds. Pour in the cream and bring to the boil, adding salt and pepper to taste, and allow to reduce for a couple of minutes until thickened.

Pour the sauce over the veggies and polenta, scatter with rosemary, and serve.

VEGAN: Plant-based double cream works well here; you could omit or swap the Parmesan for plant-based, and switch out the butter for olive oil.
GF: Yes.
SEASONAL SWAPS: This works so well as a template all year round; try beetroot (beet) and carrots, or potatoes and spring cabbage wedges instead of the aubergines.

CAULIFLOWER WITH CHICKPEAS, POMEGRANATE + TAHINI YOGHURT

Bring this impressive delight to the table, wisps of steam rising from the dome, the scent of spice filling the air, and you'll have a room full of anticipation. The crucial thing is judging the cooking of the cauliflower: the first half with foil covering, the second without, gets you there with the right amount of scorching, and a cake tester helps judge the correct resistance still left in the cauli.

You don't have to use baking parchment on the top before wrapping in foil, but it means more of the spiced yoghurt remains on the cauliflower.

Serves 4

75g (2½oz) yoghurt
3 tbsp chilli paste
1 whole cauliflower, largest leaves removed
3 tbsp extra virgin olive oil
400g (14oz) can chickpeas, drained and rinsed
1 red onion, thinly sliced
1 pomegranate, seeds only
small bunch of coriander (cilantro), leaves chopped
generous pinch of ground cumin
flaky sea salt and freshly ground black pepper
flatbreads, to serve (see page 183 for homemade)

For the tahini yoghurt
60g (2¼oz) tahini
60ml (4 tbsp) water
juice of ½ lemon
1 garlic clove, crushed
75g (2½oz) yoghurt
salt, to taste

Preheat the oven to 200°C/180°C fan/400°F.

In a small bowl, mix the yoghurt and chilli paste together.

Season the cauliflower with salt and pepper, place on a baking tray and brush the yoghurt and chilli mixture evenly over the cauliflower. Loosely place a piece of baking parchment over the cauliflower and cover tightly with foil.

Roast for 25 minutes, then remove the foil and baking parchment lid and add the olive oil, chickpeas and onion to the tray. Cook for another 15 minutes until the cauliflower is tender (check by pushing a skewer into the centre) and golden.

Whisk all the tahini yoghurt ingredients together in a bowl and add salt to taste, adding more water if needed to reach the consistency of thick double (heavy) cream.

Pour half the sauce over the cauliflower, then sprinkle with the pomegranate seeds, coriander and cumin. Serve with flatbreads and the rest of the sauce on the side.

VEGAN: Use plant-based yoghurt.
GF: Yes.
SEASONAL SWAPS: The combination of roasted veg, tahini sauce, pomegranates and so on works well with so many roasted vegetables, though for most I'd be inclined to omit the chilli/yoghurt covering. Try carrots, parsnips and celeriac, or aubergine (eggplant) and/or sweet potato wedges, in place of the cauliflower.

CAULIFLOWER + BROCCOLI CHEESE

My daughter has always had a deep attachment to cauliflower cheese, which I don't mind, but as a founding member of the Church of Eternal Crunch, I find it can get a little uni-textural. The addition of pangrattato – breadcrumbs in olive oil – creates a crunchy crust that makes us both happy. I hope it works that way for you too.

Serves 4

1 medium cauliflower, cut into bite-sized florets

1 medium broccoli, cut into bite-sized florets

50g (2oz) butter

50g (2oz) plain (all-purpose) flour

800ml (1¾ pints) milk

100g (3½oz) Parmesan, grated

generous scratching of nutmeg

30g (1oz) fresh breadcrumbs

2 tbsp extra virgin olive oil

flaky sea salt and freshly ground black pepper

In a large pan of simmering water, blanch the cauliflower and broccoli florets for 3–4 minutes until just tender, then drain.

Preheat the oven to 200°C/180°C fan/400°F.

In a medium saucepan, melt the butter over a medium heat. Add the flour and stir constantly for about 1–2 minutes until thick. Slowly add the milk, whisking continuously to avoid lumps. Keep stirring until the mixture thickens and becomes smooth. Stir half the Parmesan into the sauce, season with the nutmeg and some salt and pepper to taste, then remove from the heat.

Gently fold the florets into the sauce until well coated and transfer to a baking dish, spreading out evenly. Combine the breadcrumbs and olive oil and sprinkle evenly over the cauliflower and broccoli mixture in the baking dish. Bake in the oven for 30 minutes until lightly golden and bubbling.

Turn the grill (broiler) to high and grill for about 1–3 minutes until the top is more deeply golden. Scatter with the remaining Parmesan and serve either with salad leaves – I do like lamb's lettuce here – or some delightful brassica; sprouts work perfectly.

VEGAN: Use plant-based butter and oat milk.
GF: Use GF flour and GF breadcrumbs, or omit the latter.
SEASONAL SWAPS: Works beautifully with just-undercooked vegetables such as potatoes, roasted shallots, tenderstem broccoli, diced roasted celeriac and carrot, and so on.

NUTMEG BAKED POTATOES + BOOZY MUSHROOMS

This is for those times you want a delicious supper and have just a little more energy than it takes to throw a handful of spuds in the oven, but not much more.

Simple though it may be, the nutmeg and booziness of the mushrooms makes it perfectly special. I like this with a simple, one leaf salad – likely as not, lamb's lettuce.

Serves 4

4 baking potatoes

500g (1lb 2oz) swede, peeled and chopped into 1cm (½in) dice

100ml (3½fl oz) milk

60g (2¼oz) butter, or extra virgin olive oil

freshly grated nutmeg

4 large mushrooms, thickly sliced

2 garlic cloves, finely chopped

3 tbsp masala, sherry or madeira

2 tbsp finely chopped fresh rosemary

150ml (5fl oz) double (heavy) cream

flaky sea salt and freshly ground black pepper

Preheat the oven to 200°C/180°C fan/400°F.

Bake the potatoes for about 1 hour until cooked and the skins are crisp.

Meanwhile, simmer the swede in plenty of boiling salted water until tender. Drain and season well with salt and pepper, before mashing with the milk and half the butter or olive oil.

Cut the potatoes in half and scoop out most of the flesh, leaving the skin plus a little extra, like a canoe. Roughly mash the scooped out flesh in a bowl, then combine with the swede and an overgenerous avalanche of nutmeg. Carefully scoop the mixture back into the potato canoes, place on a baking tray and cook for 10–15 minutes until golden.

Meanwhile, add the rest of the butter or oil to a large frying pan and cook the mushrooms over a medium heat with a big pinch of salt. After 5 minutes or so they'll release their liquid; at this point, add the garlic and cook for about a minute, stirring a couple of times. Add the masala and cook for 2 more minutes, then stir in the rosemary. Check the seasoning and drizzle over the cream, warming it through for a minute or so. Serve the baked potatoes with the mushrooms on the side.

VEGAN: Use plant-based cream and oat milk.
GF: Yes.
SEASONAL SWAPS: The potatoes can be replaced with sweet potatoes, the swede with carrots, parsnips, Jerusalem artichokes or celeriac, and shredded sprouts work particularly well in place of the mushrooms.

JANSSON'S MISO TEMPTATION

See how I get you past the recipe title before unveiling the turnip. The good news is turnips are delicious; they are just one in a long line of flavoursome delights that suffer from an association with poorer times. In Italy it's sweet chestnuts, in the UK it's turnips. The classic Jansson's has a central layer of onions and anchovies, the deeply flavoured filling in a kind of dauphinoise sandwich; this version tumbles the whole together, the crucial savouriness beautifully provided by the porcini and miso, with a final flourish of seaweed.

Serve with a salad in summer, or green vegetables in cooler weather.

Serves 4

15g (½oz) dried porcini
30g (1oz) butter
1 large onion, thinly sliced
800g (1lb 12oz) waxy small or new potatoes, washed but unpeeled
400g (14oz) small turnips
200ml (7fl oz) whole milk
150ml (5fl oz) double (heavy) cream
30g (1oz) white miso
1–2 tsp dried seaweed flakes (optional)
flaky sea salt and freshly ground black pepper

Preheat the oven to 200°C/180°C fan/400°F.

Soak the porcini in 150ml (5fl oz) kettle-hot water for 5 minutes, then remove the mushrooms, reserving the soaking liquid.

Melt the butter in a medium pan over a medium heat, add the onion and cook for 10 minutes, stirring often, until soft but not browned.

Meanwhile, slice the potatoes and turnips about 5mm (¼in) thick and combine with the milk and cream in a large bowl.

Stir the mushrooms and miso through the soft onions, then add 100ml (3½fl oz) of the mushroom soaking liquid, leaving any residue or grit behind.

Stir the mushroomy onions through the potato and turnip mix and season with salt and pepper. Layer into a baking dish, cover with foil and cook for 20 minutes, then uncover and bake for 20–30 minutes, or until the potatoes and turnips are fully cooked and browning at the edges. Add a splash of milk while it cooks if it's looking a bit dry.

Allow to rest for 5 minutes before serving sprinkled with the dried seaweed flakes (if using).

VEGAN: Use plant-based cream and milk.
GF: Yes.
SEASONAL SWAPS: This is extraordinary with just potatoes, parsnips, Jerusalem artichokes, celeriac and many other root vegetables. Yes, even beetroot (beet) on its own.

Curr

ies and Stews

GIGANTES PLAKI

This Greek classic may have beans – traditionally dried giant white beans (aka gigantes) – at its heart, but it shows as well as any recipe the brilliance of that coming together of tomatoes, celery, carrot, garlic and onions in building depth of flavour, and with it deep satisfaction. Two shortcuts are possible: availability is likely to have you swapping giant white beans for butter beans, and you can use canned rather than dried – they will work perfectly well, but flavours penetrate dried beans more than canned. If you grow them, do try this with borlotti beans; they work beautifully.

Serves 4

300g (10oz) butter (lima) beans

60ml (4 tbsp) extra virgin olive oil

1 onion, finely chopped

2 garlic cloves, finely chopped

1 carrot, peeled and finely chopped

3 celery sticks, finely chopped

1 cinnamon stick

1 tbsp tomato purée (paste)

400g (14oz) can chopped tomatoes

1 tsp sugar

4 sprigs of flat leaf parsley, stalks reserved, leaves finely chopped

1 tsp dried oregano

2 bay leaves

flaky sea salt and freshly ground black pepper

To serve

toast

feta

extra virgin olive oil

dried oregano

If you are using dried beans, soak them overnight in a large bowl covered with water. Drain and rinse.

Preheat the oven to 180°C/160°C fan/350°F.

Heat the oil in a medium casserole dish over a medium heat, add the onion, garlic, carrot and celery and cook, stirring often, for 10 minutes until softened.

Add the cinnamon stick, tomato purée, tomatoes, sugar, parsley stalks, dried oregano, bay leaves and a generous amount of black pepper. Simmer for about 10 minutes until thick. Add the beans and mix well to coat, adding enough water to just cover them.

Cover with a lid or tightly with foil and bake for 1½–2 hours, checking after an hour and adding more water if needed to prevent drying out.

Remove from the oven, stir through the chopped parsley leaves and season if needed. Remove the bay leaves and parsley stalks.

Serve with toast and crumbled feta, drizzled with a little olive oil and sprinkled with oregano.

VEGAN: Use vegan feta.
GF: Serve with GF bread.
SEASONAL SWAPS: You can alter this by adding finely diced squash, celeriac or Jerusalem artichokes with, or instead of, the carrot.

CAPONATA

This Sicilian delight shares a lot in the way of sensibility with the summer pasta salad on page 96, both taking the best of summer's sun-loving vegetables and sitting them with an agrodolce (sweet/sour) dressing, with olives, capers and pine nuts as backing singers. A handful of dried fruit in this dish works perfectly too, if you fancy it.

There are endless variations even to the cooking method – some allow this to simmer for an hour, or to bake in the oven – and as delightful as that may be, I most often fancy the fresher result this gives.

I'd be very inclined to eat this with toasted sourdough or ciabatta rubbed with garlic and swizzled with olive oil.

Serves 4

2 aubergines (eggplants), cut into bite-sized pieces

4 tbsp extra virgin olive oil, plus more to drizzle

1 onion, finely chopped

4 celery sticks, finely chopped

1 red (bell) pepper, finely chopped

2 garlic cloves, finely chopped

400g (14oz) cherry tomatoes, halved

2 tbsp red wine vinegar

1 tsp sugar

80g (3oz) pitted green olives, roughly chopped

2 tbsp capers, drained and rinsed

bunch of fresh basil, leaves picked

2 tbsp pine nuts, toasted

flaky sea salt and freshly ground black pepper

Dissolve 1 tablespoon salt in 1 litre (2 pints) water and soak the diced aubergine for about 30 minutes. Drain well and pat dry with a clean tea towel.

Heat 2 tablespoons of the oil in a large frying pan or skillet over a medium heat. Add the aubergine and cook until browned and softened, stirring occasionally. Remove to a bowl.

In the same pan, add the remaining olive oil and cook the onion, celery and red pepper for 7–10 minutes, stirring occasionally, until softened. Add the garlic and cook for another minute.

Stir in the tomatoes and cook for 7 minutes or so until softened and collapsed. Add the vinegar and sugar and cook for a couple of minutes until the liquid has cooked away. Stir in the cooked aubergine, green olives, capers, half the basil and the pine nuts and season to taste with salt and pepper. Remove from the heat.

Serve at room temperature with a drizzle more olive oil and scattered with the remaining basil.

VEGAN: Yes.
GF: Yes.
SEASONAL SWAPS: This is a celebration of late summer vegetables, but by all means try it with courgettes (zucchini) or larger tomatoes, or swap the pine nuts for almonds.

VIGNAROLA

This light Roman stew celebrates so much of what is special about spring – the first small artichokes, early peas and broad beans, and a handful of spring onions – but later in the year, when the next wave of globe artichokes comes through, and even into autumn, you can make this with frozen peas and beans if you fancy. Porcini mushrooms are not essential – they bring depth of flavour that dilutes the brightness – but I like them here. Make this as is, then tweak to suit if you fancy. If you have a bottle open, you can replace half the stock with white wine if you like.

Serves 4

½ lemon

4 globe artichokes

4 tbsp extra virgin olive oil, plus a drizzle to serve

2 garlic cloves, thinly sliced

20g (¾oz) dried porcini mushrooms, finely chopped

bunch of spring onions (scallions), thinly sliced

4 sprigs of mint, half the leaves finely chopped, half left whole

4 sprigs of parsley, half the leaves finely chopped, half left whole

150ml (5fl oz) vegetable stock (page 192, or use good shop-bought)

200g (7oz) fresh peas

200g (7oz) fresh broad (fava) beans

flaky sea salt and freshly ground black pepper

toast, to serve

Fill a bowl with water and squeeze the juice of the lemon half into it. Trim the artichokes by removing the tough outer leaves, cutting off the tops and scooping out the choke. Cut them into four or eight (depending on size) and immediately place them in the lemon water to prevent browning.

Heat the olive oil in a large pan over a medium heat, add the garlic, drained artichokes, porcini and thinly sliced spring onions and cook for 5 minutes until they're softened. Add the whole herbs and the vegetable stock and cover and cook for 10–15 minutes until the artichokes are tender and the sauce is thick.

Add the peas and broad beans to the pan and cook for 2–3 minutes. Season to taste, then mix in the finely chopped herbs and top with a drizzle of olive oil. Serve warm or at room temperature, with toast.

VEGAN: Yes.
GF: Serve with GF toast.
SEASONAL SWAPS: This is, by definition, a stew of spring vegetables that suits the warmer months of the year, so while the opportunities for seasonal variation are limited, you could try this with green beans, runner beans, asparagus and so on, if you like.

SPRING INTO SUMMER LAKSA

You'll have no trouble finding this wonderful, spicy noodle soup in much of south Asia – it's even the national dish in Malaysia and Singapore – and there are as many variations of it as there are islands in the surrounding seas. It is usual to include prawns, shrimp and pork, perhaps tofu too, but I don't miss any of them in this vegetable-heavy version.

The ingredients are numerous but the process is simple; make it once, and it'll be your friend for life. This version takes advantage of the best vegetables spring-into-summer has to offer. As ever, it is highly adaptable.

Serves 4

For the paste

2 tbsp light soy sauce

3 garlic cloves, roughly chopped

2 tbsp grated fresh ginger

1 tsp ground turmeric

1 tsp ground cumin

2 tsp ground coriander

½ tsp ground black pepper

½–1 tsp chilli powder

3 lemongrass stalks, roughly chopped

½ small bunch of coriander (cilantro), leaves only, chopped

For the laksa

3 tbsp extra virgin olive oil

1 litre (2 pints) vegetable stock (page 192, or use good shop-bought)

2 tbsp tamarind paste

400ml (14fl oz) can coconut milk

2 limes

1 tsp sugar, or more to taste

soy sauce, to taste

200g (7oz) thin rice noodles, ready-cooked or cooked and drained as per the packet instructions

100g (3½oz) beansprouts

30g (1oz) pea shoots

150g (5oz) green beans, thinly sliced

100g (3½fl oz) baby spinach, thinly sliced

150g (5oz) radishes, thinly sliced (add the thinly sliced leaves if you have them)

½ cucumber, cut into matchsticks

small bunch each of coriander (cilantro), mint and/or Thai basil, leaves chopped

1–3 bird's-eye chillies, thinly sliced

Put all the ingredients for the paste into a blender and blitz to a coarse paste, adding a splash of water if required.

Heat the olive oil in a pan over a medium heat and fry the paste for 2–3 minutes until it just begins to stick to the pan. Add the stock, tamarind and coconut milk and bring to the boil. Season with the juice of one of the limes, the sugar and more soy sauce to taste.

Divide the noodles between four bowls, add the vegetables and pour the hot broth over. Serve immediately, sprinkled with plenty of herbs and sliced chilli, and with lime wedges on the side for squeezing over.

VEGAN: Yes.

GF: Use GF soy sauce.

SEASONAL SWAPS: Earlier in spring you should try this with asparagus rather than green beans; later in summer you might fancy shredded courgettes (zucchini) rather than cucumber, and runner beans rather than green beans.

LEEKS WITH TARRAGON PUY LENTILS

If ever a bowl of delicious comfort existed, this is it. Warm, herby lentils, perfectly dressed, with thick, squeaky, sweet leeks might just be worth the short days and dipping temperatures that suit it so well. Truth is, this is as delicious as a salad in summer too, and you can use other lentils – green or brown work especially well – if you fancy. If you find yourself without date syrup, try honey or pomegranate molasses; it'll be different but equally good.

Serves 4

300g (10oz) Puy (French) lentils

2 bay leaves

8 garlic cloves: 6 finely chopped, 2 peeled and left whole

80ml (3fl oz) extra virgin olive oil

3 large leeks, trimmed and cut into 4cm (1½in) lengths and washed well

2 tbsp date syrup

juice of 1 lemon

small bunch of tarragon, leaves picked

flaky sea salt and freshly ground black pepper

Rinse the lentils and put in a pan with the bay leaves and the whole garlic cloves and just cover with water. Bring to the boil, skim off any froth that surfaces, then simmer for 20 minutes, add ½ teaspoon salt and cook for 5–10 minutes longer until the lentils are cooked through but still with slight resistance.

Heat half the olive oil in a medium pan over a medium heat and add the leeks along with a big pinch of salt and pepper. Turn the heat down to low, cover the pan and cook gently for 15–20 minutes, stirring halfway through, until the leeks are tender.

In a small frying pan, cook the chopped garlic in the rest of the olive oil for 2 minutes until just golden; don't let the colour darken to brown. Remove from the heat and stir in the date syrup and the lemon juice, adding salt and pepper to taste.

Drain the lentils, discarding the bay leaves and whole garlic cloves. Stir the date syrup dressing and half the tarragon through the lentils and serve warm, scattered with the rest of the tarragon and the leeks.

VEGAN: Yes.
GF: Yes.
SEASONAL SWAPS: Leeks are available for much of the year, but if you fancy a change, try shallots, red or white onions, or globe artichoke hearts.

CELERY, ONION + WHITE BEAN STEW

Thank heavens for celery's shelf life. Buy a head to use a stalk or two for soup, and chances are the rest is still in good order a fortnight later when you need more. Celery is so often like that most excellent of friends who helps, advises, consoles and generally lifts others, who even if its presence isn't obvious, is there so that everything else can shine. Here, it most certainly is present, its earthy bitterness perfect against the buttery sweetness of beans and onions. Serve with greens and/or excellent bread.

Serves 4

2 heads of celery, leaves cut off and reserved, the base and any rough outer stalks removed

60g (2¼oz) butter

2 onions, finely chopped

4 garlic cloves, finely chopped

small sprig of thyme

2 bay leaves

150ml (5fl oz) white wine

150ml (5fl oz) vegetable stock (page 192, or use good shop-bought)

200ml (7fl oz) double (heavy) cream

2 x 400g (14oz) cans cannellini or butter (lima) beans, drained and rinsed

big pinch of grated nutmeg

4–5 cooked chestnuts (if you have them)

flaky sea salt and freshly ground black pepper

Preheat the oven to 190°C/170°C fan/375°F.

Slice all the celery stalks into 3cm (1¼in) pieces at an angle. Melt the butter in a large, heavy-based casserole over a low-medium heat, add the celery and onions with the garlic, thyme and bay leaves and cook for 10–15 minutes until softened.

Add the wine and simmer vigorously for 2–3 minutes until the wine reduces by half. Add the stock and a good pinch of salt and pepper and bring to a simmer, then cover with the lid and cook in the centre of the oven for 25–30 minutes until completely tender.

Meanwhile, blend or very finely chop the celery leaves with 2 teaspoons coarse or flaky sea salt to create a wet mix.

Add the cream, white beans and nutmeg to the stew, return to the hob and bring to a simmer. Cook for 5 minutes until thickened, then season generously with pepper and more nutmeg if needed. Remove the thyme sprig. Serve with the chestnuts finely grated over the top and with a big pinch of the celery salt.

VEGAN: Use plant-based cream and olive oil instead of butter.
GF: Yes.
SEASONAL SWAPS: This is a celebration of celery, so by all means use something with similar bitterness like chicory (endive) or celeriac instead.

CAULIFLOWER, SPINACH + POTATO CURRY

It's good to have a few curry recipes, each with a distinct character, to call on when the deep, often urgent need for spices calls at your door. This – simple and balanced as it is – should be one of that handful. The warm, earthy spices set the tone, with the degree of chilli heat entirely up to you.

Serves 4

3 tbsp ghee or coconut oil

1 tsp cumin seeds

1 tsp mustard seeds

300g (10oz) small onions or shallots, peeled but left whole

3 garlic cloves, finely chopped

1 tbsp finely grated fresh ginger

2–4 slim green chillies

3 tomatoes, finely chopped

1 tsp ground turmeric

1 tsp ground coriander

1 tsp ground cumin

½ tsp red chilli powder or flakes (or more to taste)

800g (1lb 12oz) waxy potatoes, cut into bite-sized pieces if large

1 small cauliflower, cut into florets

200g (7oz) spinach leaves

2 tsp garam masala

1 tsp fenugreek leaf (optional)

flaky sea salt and freshly ground black pepper

small bunch of coriander (cilantro), finely chopped, to serve

cooked rice, to serve

Heat the ghee or oil in a large pan over a medium heat. Add the cumin seeds and mustard seeds and cook until they pop and sizzle. Add the onions and cook, stirring occasionally, for 7–10 minutes until they begin to colour, then add the garlic, ginger and whole green chillies and cook for about 30 seconds.

Add the chopped tomatoes, the ground turmeric, coriander and cumin and the chilli powder and cook for a few minutes. Add the potatoes and cauliflower and pour in enough water to just cover, then season with salt. Cover and cook for 10 minutes, then uncover and continue to cook until the potatoes and cauliflower are tender.

Stir in the spinach and allow to wilt, then add the garam masala and fenugreek leaf (if using) and season to taste with salt and pepper.

Sprinkle with the coriander leaves and serve with rice.

VEGAN: Yes, with coconut oil instead of ghee.
GF: Yes.
SEASONAL SWAPS: The three main vegetables are available all year round, but if you fancy something different, use this as a template for a similar weight of whichever combination of sweet potatoes, chickpeas, aubergines (eggplants), peas and squash you fancy.

CARROT, PRUNE + BARLEY STEW

There's a Persian fish stew in my book *Sour* that might be the recipe I fancy most when summer is leaning into autumn and – in the way you don't want to play your favourite album to death, but it's good to listen to something like it – I've taken its gently sour, spicy spirit and twisted it into this simple but so satisfying autumnal stew.

Serves 4

12 small to medium carrots, peeled and cut in half

4 tbsp extra virgin olive oil

1 onion, finely chopped

3 garlic cloves, thinly sliced

2 tsp ground cumin

1 tsp ground coriander

½ tsp ground turmeric

big pinch ground cinnamon

2 black limes, pierced a few times with a knife (or use 1 tsp dried lime flakes or 1 tsp sumac)

150g (5oz) pearl barley

900ml (2 pints) vegetable stock (page 192, or use good shop-bought)

12 large pitted prunes

juice of 1 lemon

small bunch of fresh dill, roughly chopped

flaky sea salt and freshly ground black pepper

Preheat the oven to 190°C/170°C fan/375°F.

Mix the carrots with 1 tablespoon of the olive oil and some salt and pepper and arrange on a baking tray. Cover with foil and roast for 10 minutes, then uncover and cook for another 10–15 minutes until tender and lightly coloured.

Heat the remaining olive oil in a large pan over a medium heat, add the onion and cook for 10 minutes until soft. Add the garlic and spices (including the black limes, if you have them) and cook for 1 minute.

Stir in the pearl barley and cook for 2 minutes, stirring a couple of times. Add the vegetable stock and prunes and bring to the boil. Reduce the heat to low, cover the pan with a lid and let it simmer for about 20 minutes until the barley is tender.

Stir in the carrots and lemon juice, then taste and add salt and pepper as needed. Scatter with the dill and serve while hot.

VEGAN: Yes.

GF: Use quinoa instead of the pearl barley.

SEASONAL SWAPS: By all means, switch the carrots for parsnips, potatoes, asparagus and so on.

AUBERGINE CURRY

This curry is beyond simple and – I promise – as quick and delicious as you'd like a curry to be on a Thursday evening when you just want the weekend to arrive. Of course, you can make your own Thai red curry paste, but if you can't be bothered, no one's judging; there are many excellent jarred versions.

Serve this with rice or flatbreads (page 183) if you fancy, but often as not it'll be rice noodles for me.

Serves 4

coconut oil, for frying

2 aubergines (eggplants), cut into bite-sized wedges

juice of 1 lime

1 tbsp extra virgin olive oil

2 garlic cloves, thinly sliced

2 tbsp finely grated fresh ginger

1 onion, thinly sliced

1 red (bell) pepper, sliced

400ml (14fl oz) can coconut milk

3 tbsp Thai red curry paste

1 tbsp soy sauce or coconut aminos

1 tbsp palm sugar or brown sugar

small bunch of Thai basil leaves

good handful of cashews

1 red chilli, thinly sliced

1 lime, cut into wedges

flaky sea salt, to taste

Heat the coconut oil in a deep pan or wok over a medium-high heat. Fry the aubergine pieces in batches until golden and crisp. Use a slotted spoon to transfer them to a plate lined with kitchen paper to absorb the excess oil. Sprinkle with salt to taste and squeeze over the lime juice.

Heat the olive oil in a large pan over a medium heat. Add the garlic and ginger and cook for about a minute until fragrant. Add the onion and red pepper and stir-fry for a couple of minutes until they start to soften. Add the coconut milk, curry paste, soy sauce and palm or brown sugar and stir well. Bring to a simmer and cook for about 5 minutes until rich and thick.

Add the aubergine and gently stir to coat with the sauce. Simmer for 2–3 minutes.

Serve scattered with the Thai basil leaves, cashews and red chilli, with lime wedges on the side.

VEGAN: Yes – choose a curry paste without shrimp paste or fish sauce.
GF: Yes – use a GF curry paste and GF soy sauce.
SEASONAL SWAPS: If you are in a rush or overcome with idleness yet want a delicious curry, use leftover cooked vegetables, boiled eggs and frozen peas instead of the fried aubergines. Coriander (cilantro) in place of the Thai basil is differently marvellous.

MATTAR PANEER

Widely used in Indian cooking, paneer is a non-melting mild cheese with a beautifully soft bite that suits the contrast of crunch, in this case provided by sugar snaps or other in-the-pod peas. It also has that joyful characteristic of taking on flavours readily. Mattar paneer is from northern India and I like it slightly drier – as here – than some make it; if you prefer more sauce, add a splash more water when cooking. I love this equally with flatbreads (page 183) or rice. And very often both.

Serves 4

400g (14oz) paneer, cut into bite-sized pieces

½–1 tsp chilli powder (or more or less to taste)

2 tsp ground turmeric

2 tsp ground coriander

2 tsp ground cumin

60g (2¼oz) ghee or butter

2 tsp cumin seeds

1 tsp mustard seeds

2–4 whole green chillies

1 onion, finely chopped

4 garlic cloves, finely chopped

2 tbsp finely grated fresh ginger

400g (14oz) can chopped tomatoes

400g (14oz) snow peas, sugar snaps or mangetout (or use peas)

50g (2oz) natural yoghurt (not Greek)

1 tsp garam masala

1 tsp fenugreek leaves, fresh (optional)

flaky sea salt and freshly ground black pepper

Dust the paneer with half the ground spices and a good pinch of salt.

Heat half the ghee in a medium frying pan over a medium heat and add the paneer. Cook the pieces, turning often, until lightly golden, then remove from the pan and set aside. Wipe out the pan.

Add the remaining ghee to the pan and cook the cumin and mustard seeds for a minute or so until they begin to pop. Add the whole green chillies, onion, garlic and ginger and cook for 5 minutes, stirring frequently, until softened. Add the other half of the ground spices and ½ teaspoon salt and cook for 30 seconds, then add the tomatoes and allow to cook for 10 minutes until thickened.

Stir in the paneer, 350ml (12fl oz) water and the peas. Simmer for 5–10 minutes, stirring occasionally, until the peas are just tender, then stir in the yoghurt. Check the seasoning and serve sprinkled with the garam masala and fenugreek leaves (if you have them).

VEGAN: This works well with firm tofu instead of the paneer; and with plant-based yoghurt, and olive oil in place of butter.
GF: Yes.
SEASONAL SWAPS: As well as using tofu instead of paneer, try vegetables with some crunch, such as thinly sliced (bell) pepper, carrot and baby sweetcorn instead of the peas.

MOLE WITH ROASTED SQUASH + RED ONION

As much as I love roasted squash – and roasted onions, for that matter – it can tend towards the sweetly one-dimensional. The antidote is choosing excellent varieties when you can – Uchiki Kuri and Crown Prince are two beauties – and pairing them with big contrasting flavours. Mole (pronounced moh-lay), a Mexican sauce made with chillies, seeds and spices, brings rich, earthy heat in the most exquisite manner. If you are new to making mole, it may appear to be a faff but please try this once, for that is all you need to bring it into your repertoire of pleasing suppers.

Serves 4

For the squash

800g (1lb 12oz) butternut squash, or other squash, cut into wedges

3 tbsp extra virgin olive oil

1 red onion, cut into wedges

4 tbsp pumpkin seeds

flaky sea salt and freshly ground black pepper

For the mole

2 dried ancho chillies

2 dried pasilla chillies

3 medium tomatoes

1 red onion, unpeeled and cut into 6 wedges

6 garlic cloves, unpeeled and whole

50g (2oz) raisins

1 tsp ground cinnamon

1 tsp oregano (Mexican oregano if you have it)

½ tsp ground allspice

½ tsp ground cumin

1 tbsp sesame seeds

2 tbsp extra virgin olive oil

Preheat the oven to 220°C/ 200°C fan/425°F.

Drizzle the squash with the olive oil, season with plenty of salt and pepper and place on a baking tray with the onion wedges. Bake for about 30 minutes, or until tender, adding the pumpkin seeds after 20 minutes.

Meanwhile, make the mole. Remove the stems and seeds of the chillies, then toast them in a dry frying pan over a medium heat for 1 minute to develop the flavour. Remove, add to a bowl and cover with boiling water, then leave to soak.

Place the pan back over a medium heat, then dry-fry the tomatoes, onion wedges and garlic cloves for 10 minutes until the skins are charred and the flesh is soft. Remove from the heat; and when cool enough to handle, peel and discard the charred skins.

Put the vegetables, chillies (discard the soaking liquid), raisins, 100ml (3½fl oz) water, the spices, sesame seeds and ½ teaspoon salt into a blender and blitz to a smooth sauce. Return the frying pan to a medium heat, add the oil and then the blitzed sauce and cook for 5 minutes until most of the liquid has evaporated and the sauce is just beginning to brown and stick to the bottom of the pan. Stir 250ml (9fl oz) water into the mole and cook for 10 minutes, or until the sauce is thick.

Spread the mole on individual plates or a platter and top with the squash, onions and pumpkin seeds. Serve as is, or with rice and/or flatbreads.

VEGAN: Yes.
GF: Yes.
SEASONAL SWAPS: This is adaptable to whichever seasonal vegetables you wish to roast to go with the mole. The chilli varieties I've used for the mole are classics of Mexican cooking, and while distinct, both have a mildish, sweet, rich and raisiny flavour. They are widely available online if you can't find them locally.

Sn

all bits

ASPARAGUS + RUNNY BOILED EGGS

I know this is so simple it's almost not a recipe, but it is here to remind you to make it – and to make it often – in spring. As ever, the freshness of the asparagus is crucial, as is the runniness of the eggs. Do try different spices: I love this with a generous pinch of paprika, garam masala or even curry powder.

Serves 4

4 eggs

2–3 bunches of asparagus, trimmed

flaky sea salt and freshly cracked black pepper

cayenne pepper

Bring a large pan of salted water to the boil. Lower the eggs in and simmer for 4–5 minutes.

Cook the asparagus in a large pan of salted water until tender, 1–3 minutes depending on their thickness.

Drain the asparagus. Serve with the eggs with the tops removed in egg cups. Dip a spear of asparagus in the egg, then in the seasonings, and eat.

VEGAN: Substitute the eggs for one or more of the dips on pages 178–9.
GF: Yes.
SEASONAL SWAPS: Fat, squeaky stems of sprouting broccoli, crisp roasted spring onions (scallions) and chips (fries) are three of the many you can swap in for the asparagus.

SPRING ON TOAST

As much as I love lettuce in a salad, I care for it equally in soup (lettuce, pea and mint is one of my favourites) and fried. If you have yet to try either, let this be the gateway to eating fried lettuce. Firm types, such as little gem, work best: the crisp core and softened – perhaps slightly burnt – edges give such a fine contrast. The smoky bitterness of the paprika sets it off perfectly, but I often make this with Aleppo pepper or other mild chilli flakes.

As ever, adapt this as you fancy: warmed butter (lima) beans or sliced green beans are among the many superb swaps for the peas and broad beans.

One of my favourite simple lunches or lazy suppers.

Serves 2–4

4 little gem lettuce, cut into 4 wedges

2 bunches of spring onions (scallions), trimmed

4 tbsp olive oil, plus more for drizzling

250g (9oz) cooked peas

250g (9oz) cooked broad (fava) beans

4 thick slices of sourdough bread

1 garlic clove, halved

small handful of mint leaves, finely shredded

generous pinch or two of smoked paprika

½ lemon, for squeezing

flaky sea salt and freshly ground black pepper

Toss the little gem wedges and spring onions in a bowl with a big pinch of salt, black pepper and 2 tablespoons of the olive oil.

Heat a large frying pan and add the little gem and spring onions and griddle for 5–8 minutes until nicely coloured and wilted. Add the peas and broad beans to the pan and heat them through for a few minutes, stirring once or twice.

Toast the bread and rub with the cut side of the garlic. Pile the vegetables on top, sprinkle with the mint and paprika, then finish with a drizzle of olive oil and a squeeze of lemon.

VEGAN: Yes.
GF: Use GF bread.
SEASONAL SWAPS: The lettuce and onions are year-round favourites, but do try this with green beans and asparagus, or halved cherry tomatoes and flash-fried courgettes (zucchini) in summer and autumn.

ASPARAGUS + WATERCRESS MIMOSA

A mimosa – a simple coming together of vegetables, grated boiled egg and lively flavours – has no right to be as sustaining as it is, and yet…

The freshness of the asparagus is crucial – essentially, this is a poem to its magnificence – so if you can make this on the same day as the asparagus is cut, you will taste the difference. Under no circumstances waste your time with the woody green pencils of Peru; it'd be like watching *A Matter of Life and Death* having clingfilmed the telly.

Serves 2–4

4 eggs

2–3 bunches of asparagus, trimmed of woody ends

1 shallot, very finely chopped

1 tbsp Dijon mustard

juice and finely grated zest of ½ lemon

3 tbsp extra virgin olive oil

small handful of watercress

1 tbsp capers

5 sprigs of tarragon, leaves roughly chopped

3 chive flowers, broken into florets (optional)

flaky sea salt and freshly ground black pepper

Boil the eggs in a pan of boiling water for 9 minutes. Drain, then run cold water into the pan for a minute or so to stop the cooking process.

Cook the asparagus in a large pan of salted water until tender, 1–3 minutes depending on their thickness.

Meanwhile, whisk the shallot, mustard, lemon juice and a big pinch of salt together in a large bowl, then whisk in the olive oil.

When the eggs are cool, peel them and discard the shells.

Drain the asparagus, add to the bowl of dressing and toss with the watercress. Season with salt and pepper. Lay on a large plate or dish, then finely grate the eggs over the top. Scatter over the capers, tarragon, chive flowers (if using) and lemon zest. Season well with salt and pepper.

VEGAN: Try fried mushrooms in place of the boiled eggs.
GF: Yes.
SEASONAL SWAPS: Sprouting broccoli, tenderstem broccoli, and leeks are among the many vegetables you can switch in for the asparagus.

FIVE DIPS

Since the age of six, it has taken a very great deal to coax me out of the house when there's a test match on. It can be sunny as you like, and the cricket will always win, especially if it's the Ashes.

I make an exception – short, but nevertheless – for a tableful of summer dips, excellent flatbreads (page 183), something cold and sparkling to drink and excellent company that knows when to leave.

All of this is gluten-free (choose bread to suit), and you can switch in vegan feta and plant-based yoghurt to great effect. Each happily serves 2 for dipping – if making all four dips, they collectively serve 4–6. *Pictured overleaf.*

TOMATO, CAPER + FETA DIP

3 large tomatoes, cut in half

2 tbsp extra virgin olive oil, plus more to drizzle

4 tbsp capers, drained

1 garlic clove, crushed

pinch of chilli flakes

½ bunch of flat-leaf parsley, finely chopped

50g (2oz) feta, crumbled

flaky sea salt and freshly ground black pepper

Preheat the oven to 200°C/180°C fan/350°F.

Place the tomatoes on a baking sheet and roast for about 15–20 minutes until soft. Remove from the oven and let them cool. When cool enough to handle, peel and remove most of the seeds.

In a food processor or blender, pulse the tomato, olive oil, capers, garlic and chilli flakes to a coarse purée. Stir in half the parsley and add salt and pepper to taste.

Transfer to a serving bowl and scatter with the rest of the parsley, the feta and a drizzle of olive oil.

BABA GANOUSH

2 large aubergines (eggplants)

juice of 1 lemon

2 tbsp tahini

1 garlic clove, crushed

2 tbsp extra virgin olive oil

generous dusting of smoked paprika

flaky sea salt and freshly ground black pepper

Cook the aubergines on the hob and drain, as described for the Aubergine kedgeree on page 91.

Scoop out the flesh, discarding the skins. In a serving bowl, stir the lemon juice into the tahini until it loosens. Add the garlic and half the olive oil. Mash in the aubergines gently, season to taste, then drizzle with the remaining olive oil and dust with smoked paprika.

RED PEPPER DIP

2 red (bell) peppers

1 garlic clove, crushed

75g (2½oz) flaked almonds (or walnuts), toasted, plus a few to serve

2 tbsp extra virgin olive oil, plus more to drizzle

1 tsp ground cumin

juice of ½ lemon

flaky sea salt

1 tsp Urfa pepper

Blacken the peppers over a gas hob or barbecue (or under a grill/broiler), turning regularly with tongs, until completely charred and collapsed. Allow to cool. Cut in half and scrape as much of the skin off as possible. Cut out the seedy core and discard along with the skin.

Using a pestle and mortar or food processor, blend the peppers, garlic, almonds, oil, cumin and lemon juice until smooth. Taste and add salt if needed. Spoon into a bowl and top with a little olive oil, a few flaked almonds and the Urfa pepper.

COURGETTE DIP

2 medium courgettes (zucchini), coarsely grated

3 tbsp extra virgin olive oil

juice of ½ lemon

1 garlic clove, crushed

50g (2oz) walnuts, roughly crushed

150g (5oz) Greek yoghurt

2 spring onions (scallions), very thinly sliced

flaky sea salt and freshly ground black pepper

In a large colander, combine the grated courgettes with a generous pinch of salt. Set over a bowl and leave to drain for 15 minutes. Squeeze the courgettes of as much liquid as possible.

Warm 2 tablespoons of the olive oil in a large frying pan over a medium heat, add the courgettes and fry for about 10 minutes until the liquid has evaporated and the courgettes have softened. Remove from the heat and allow to cool.

Mix in the lemon juice, garlic, half the walnuts, yoghurt and the spring onions. Taste and season if needed.

Scatter with the remaining walnuts and a drizzle of olive oil.

BROAD BEAN DIP

150g (5oz) podded fresh broad (fava) beans (use frozen if you prefer; peas are also excellent)

2 garlic cloves, thinly sliced

2 tbsp extra virgin olive oil

zest and juice of ½ lemon

10 mint leaves, roughly chopped

flaky sea salt and freshly ground black pepper

pinch of Aleppo pepper or other chilli flakes, to serve

Bring a pan of salted water to the boil and simmer the broad beans with the garlic for 4 minutes, then drain and submerge in cold water. Once cold, drain and skin any beans that are larger than a small fingernail.

Blend the beans – not too smoothly – with the olive oil, lemon zest and mint leaves. Taste and add salt, pepper and lemon juice to taste. I like this with a pinch of Aleppo pepper at the end to add a little bite.

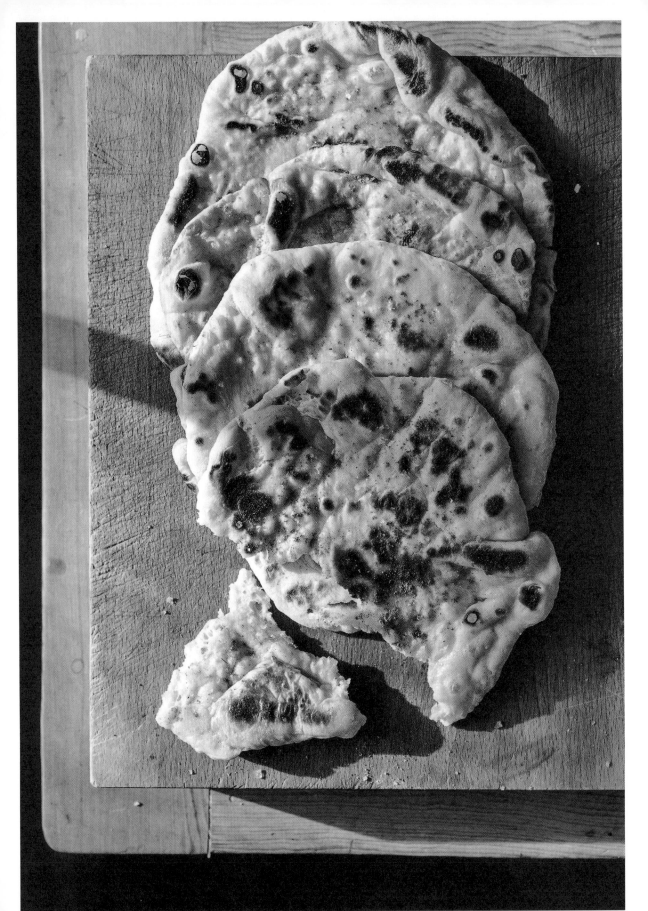

FLATBREADS

Everyone should have a brilliant flatbread recipe to turn to; here is yours. Try these with the dips on pages 178–9, any of the soups, in place of rice or potatoes with stews and curries – basically anywhere that takes your fancy. The gluten-free bread flours I've tried have all worked well here.

Makes 4

1 tsp dried yeast
3 tbsp olive oil
175ml (6oz) warm water
250g (9oz) bread flour, plus extra for dusting
⅓ tsp fine sea salt
good pinch of flaky sea salt
good pinch of garam masala (optional)

Stir the yeast, 2 tablespoons the oil and the water together in a small bowl until the yeast dissolves.

Add the flour to a large bowl, then tip in the yeast mixture and stir to combine until a rough dough forms. Cover and leave to rest for 10 minutes. Fold in the fine sea salt, cover and rest for another 10 minutes. Stretch and fold the dough, turning it 90 degrees each time, and repeating 7 times, so the dough feels tight. Cover and allow to develop in a warm place for an hour.

Cut the dough into quarters. On a lightly floured surface, roll each piece into an oval about 5mm (¼in) thick.

Cook the flatbreads, one at a time, in a hot, dry frying pan set over a medium-high heat. Cook for 2 minutes until puffed and lightly charred, then flip and cook the other side until lightly charred (another minute or so). When still warm, brush the flatbreads with the remaining olive oil and sprinkle with flaky sea salt, and garam masala if using.

VEGAN: Yes.
GF: Use GF bread flour.
SEASONAL SWAPS: Try swapping the garam masala for another of your favourite spice mixes.

AUBERGINE FRIES WITH WHIPPED FETA + DUKKAH

I have to confess that while this book is – with the exception of a few puds – full of satisfying lunches and suppers, this one is a stretch of a main course; you'll be after a side to go with it, or use it as a seriously half-time appetite satisfier. Make the whipped feta and dukkah ahead – quick in themselves – and it's only a few minutes until you are deeply pleased.

Serves 4

2 medium aubergines (eggplants), cut into 1cm (½ in) fries
1 tsp ground cumin
4 tbsp cornflour (cornstarch)
2 tbsp plain (all-purpose) flour
sunflower oil, for frying
a little pomegranate molasses
small bunch of dill, roughly chopped
flaky sea salt and freshly ground black pepper

For the whipped feta
150g (5oz) feta
100g (3½ oz) Greek yoghurt
zest and juice of ½ lemon

For the hazelnut dukkah
50g (2oz) hazelnuts
2 tbsp sesame seeds
1 tbsp coriander seeds
1 tbsp cumin seeds
½ tsp chilli flakes

Sprinkle the aubergine fries with salt and place in a colander where they'll let go of some of their water.

To make the whipped feta, in a food processor, blend the feta, yoghurt, lemon zest and juice and some black pepper until smooth. Taste and season more if needed.

Now make the dukkah. In a medium pan, lightly toast the hazelnuts and seeds over a medium heat until fragrant and slightly golden, agitating the pan often to prevent burning. Remove from the heat and let them cool. Using a pestle and mortar or a food processor, coarsely grind the hazelnuts and seeds with the chilli flakes and a big pinch of salt.

In a large bowl, mix the cumin, cornflour, plain flour, ½ teaspoon salt and some black pepper. Pat the aubergine fries dry, then toss them in the flour mixture and coat well.

Fill a deep, heavy-based pan a third full with sunflower oil and place over a medium heat. Test the heat of the oil by adding a small piece of bread; it should sizzle and turn golden. If you have a food thermometer, 180°C/350°F is a good temperature to aim for.

Fry the aubergines in batches until golden and crisp, then drain on kitchen paper and toss in half the dukkah.

Spread the whipped feta on individual plates or a platter, then top with the aubergine fries and sprinkle with pomegranate molasses, the remaining dukkah and the chopped dill.

VEGAN: Use plant-based feta and yoghurt.
GF: Use GF flour.
SEASONAL SWAPS: Try with potatoes, sweet potatoes or parsnips, bearing in mind there is no need to salt and drain as you do aubergines.

SPROUTING BROCCOLI + ROUILLE

When I lived in the city, one of the consolations of winter was the sweet grassiness of sprouting broccoli, ready after its few moments' conversation with boiling water. When I had space to grow my own, the choice of varieties meant I had getting on half the year when I could pick it, but it is in the cold months I like it best. Sit me at a table with this glossy, inky rouille, and I'll keep eating it as long as you keep serving it.

If you don't have a food processor, very finely chop the peppers and garlic and mix into the egg yolk before whisking in the oil.

Serves 4

1 large garlic clove, crushed

½ red (bell) pepper, roasted, peeled and deseeded (or use a couple of jarred piquillo peppers)

1 egg yolk

2 tsp white wine vinegar

small pinch of saffron

150ml (5fl oz) extra virgin olive oil

flaky sea salt

cayenne pepper

600–800g (1lb 5oz–1lb 12oz) sprouting broccoli, trimmed into pieces suited to dipping

Combine the garlic, red pepper, egg yolk, vinegar and saffron in the bowl of a food processor. Pulse until smooth, then slowly drizzle in the oil, just a few drops at first, then in a steady stream continuously until the rouille thickens. Season generously with salt and cayenne pepper to taste.

In a pan of boiling salted water, cook the sprouting broccoli for 2–3 minutes until just tender. Remove from the heat and drain well.

Dress the broccoli with a little of the rouille and serve with the rest on the side.

VEGAN: Use 15ml (1 tbsp) vegan egg yolk.
GF: Yes.
SEASONAL SWAPS: Try this rouille with whichever seasonal vegetables take your fancy – steamed asparagus, roasted parsnips and boiled new potatoes are three of my favourites.

BURNT LEEKS WITH ROMESCO

This utterly beguiling Spanish sauce is often made with tomatoes alongside the peppers, though I have to say, I've a deep preference for the sweetness and gentle pungency of roasted peppers on their own here: the clarity of flavour makes me happy. You can use fresh peppers – preparing them as for the red pepper dip on page 179 – or use jarred. In Spain, calçots – a kind of green onion – would be used here, but leeks (or indeed spring onions/scallions) are just wonderful. By all means switch the walnuts for almonds or hazelnuts if in season or just in your kitchen.

Serves 4

2 slices of sourdough or ciabatta, toasted, crusts removed, torn into pieces

1 garlic clove, thinly sliced

50g (2oz) flaked or whole almonds

150g (5oz) roasted, deseeded and peeled red peppers

1–3 tsp red wine vinegar or sherry vinegar

1 tsp paprika (smoked or unsmoked)

50ml (2fl oz) extra virgin olive oil, plus extra to drizzle

8 medium leeks, green end only trimmed, and washed

flaky sea salt and freshly ground black pepper

If roasting in the oven, preheat to 220°C/ 200°C fan/425°F.

Combine the bread, garlic and almonds in a food processor until coarsely ground. Add the roasted peppers, vinegar and half the paprika and process until smooth. With the processor going, add the olive oil in a thin stream until it is fully emulsified. Taste and add salt and pepper, plus more vinegar if you like.

Preheat the grill (broiler) or barbecue, if not using the oven.

Roast, grill or barbecue the leeks for 10–15 minutes, turning a couple of times, until slightly charred and cooked through.

Cut the root end of the leek off, then run a sharp knife down the length of the leek, peel away the blackened layers and remove the soft centre. Arrange them on a platter, spoon over the romesco, dust with the remaining paprika and finish with a drizzle of olive oil and some salt and pepper.

VEGAN: Yes.
GF: Use GF bread.
SEASONAL SWAPS: Try this with whichever seasonal vegetables take your fancy – steamed or grilled asparagus, roasted parsnips, carrot sticks or sprouting broccoli all go well with the romesco.

GLOBE ARTICHOKES WITH HOLLANDAISE

Eating a whole globe artichoke might just be the only meal where there is more left after you've eaten it than when you began. What starts as a tight ball of petals undergoes a soft shattering, each petal discarded once relieved of its succulent nub. Amidst the chatter and driest of white wine, it's often only at the close that you realize the mess you've made.

It can be intimidating to first tackle a cooked globe artichoke, but once familiar it is simple. Hold an outer petal and tear downwards to separate it from the whole. The part of the petal that was attached will have come away with a little nugget of glorious flesh: dip this part of the petal into the sauce and scrape it against your bottom front teeth to slip it free, discarding the tough part. Repeat, in a state of gentle wonderment, until the petals are gone. As you progress towards the tender heart, the petals become more succulent.

Serves 4

For the artichokes
juice of ½ lemon
4 large artichokes
flaky sea salt

For the hollandaise sauce
3 large egg yolks
200g (7oz) unsalted butter, melted
juice of ½ lemon
flaky sea salt and freshly ground black pepper

Add the lemon juice to a bowl of water; this stops the artichokes discolouring.

Trim the stems of each artichoke tight to the head and remove any tough outer petals. Cut off the top 1–2 centimetres of each artichoke. Rinse and add to the lemon water.

Fill a large pan with water, add salt and bring to the boil.

Place the artichokes in the pan, reduce the heat to medium and simmer for 20–30 minutes until the leaves easily pull off.

While the artichokes are cooking, prepare the hollandaise sauce. In a heatproof bowl, whisk the egg yolks until smooth. Place the bowl over a pan of gently simmering water; the bowl shouldn't touch the water. Slowly pour the melted butter in a thin stream into the egg yolks, whisking constantly until the sauce thickens. Remove the bowl from the heat. Whisk in the lemon juice and season with salt and pepper to taste.

Remove the artichokes from the pan and drain thoroughly. Serve the artichokes warm, with the hollandaise sauce on the side to dip, and a bowl for discarded petals. Napkins are your friend.

VEGAN: Instead of hollandaise, make a punchy dressing of equal parts lemon juice, excellent olive oil and Dijon mustard, with a generous pinch of salt.
GF: Yes.
SEASONAL SWAPS: Globe artichokes are available for much of the year and you can't really substitute them for anything else here, but you can use hollandaise wherever you fancy – with cooked broccoli or asparagus, for example.

VEGETABLE STOCK

I've made vegetable stock in any number of ways, but nothing comes close to the clarity of flavour here. You will get a perfectly fine result from simmering this for 45 minutes, but the short period of heat suggested below encourages the flavour to release from the ingredients without inviting the more bitter notes to the party or losing individual flavours to an amalgamated whole. Try it: I promise you will not go back. If you only use it for soups, they will elevate from yeah nice to oh my god.

This core recipe is very adaptable to what you have; I've given some guidance below about what works well and what to avoid.

**Makes about 2 litres
(4 pints)**

4 celery sticks, thickly sliced

2 leeks, thickly sliced

2 carrots, thickly sliced

1 onion, thickly sliced

2 garlic cloves, thinly sliced

1 tsp coriander seeds

1 tsp peppercorns

2 parsley stalks

2 sprigs of thyme

2 bay leaves

300ml (10fl oz) white wine (optional)

½ tsp salt

Put all of the ingredients into a large pan and cover with 2 litres (4 pints) of water. Bring to the boil, then reduce to a simmer and cook for 5 minutes. Remove from the heat and allow to cool, then place in the fridge, covered, overnight.

Pour through a sieve, pressing to extract as much flavour as possible.

This will keep in the fridge for 3 days or for 6 months in the freezer.

ADDITIONAL FLAVOURINGS

Vegetables (*especially as trimmings*):
- Mushrooms
- Fresh tomatoes (but avoid seeds)
- Fennel bulbs
- Asparagus
- Pea pods
- Celeriac
- Squash peelings

Herbs:
- Tarragon
- Chervil
- Dill

Extras:
- Fennel seeds
- Star anise
- Dried mushrooms
- Fresh ginger
- Lemongrass
- Kombu
- Parmesan rinds

Avoid:
- Members of the brassica family: broccoli, cauliflower, kale and cabbage etc.
- Starchy vegetables such as potatoes
- Beetroot (beet)
- Turnip

Unexp

ectedly
sweet

BEETROOT RICE PUDDING

For every 'excellent' idea that you can't quite nail as you'd like (yes, I'm talking about you, rhubarb curry), there is another that rewards the dedication of repeated tweaks. This, friends, is the oval intersect in the Venn diagram of beetroot risotto and chocolate beetroot brownie. You could, of course, make this without the beetroot and it would be deeply pleasurable, but beetroot's sweetness and gentle earthiness accentuates and anchors the sweeter elements of this, as it all but dissolves into the milk. It acts as much as a spice than anything.

If you fancy, sprinkle with the light brown sugar and flash this under a hot grill until a bubbling, lightly brown skin forms.

Serves 4

300g (10oz) beetroot (beet), peeled and grated

zest of 1 orange, half pared, half finely grated

2 long sprigs of rosemary

2 tsp ground cardamom

1 bay leaf, cracked

700ml (1½ pints) milk

160g (5½oz) arborio rice, washed

45g (1¾oz) caster (superfine) sugar

20g (¾oz) butter

1 tbsp soft light brown sugar

1 tbsp cocoa powder

a little double (heavy) cream, to swirl

Put the beetroot, pared orange zest, rosemary, cardamom, bay leaf and milk in a large pan and bring to a simmer. Add the rice, stir, and bring back up to the boil, then turn down to a gentle simmer. It should take 25–35 minutes for the rice to cook and the beetroot to all but dissolve. Stir in the caster sugar, then the butter and add a touch more milk if needed.

To serve, sprinkle with the brown sugar, grated orange zest and cocoa powder and swirl with cream.

VEGAN: Use plant-based cream, milk and butter.
GF: Yes.
SEASONAL SWAPS: Parsnip works really well in place of the beetroot and I'm fairly sure sweet potato would work beautifully. My guess is that celeriac and Jerusalem artichoke would too, perhaps with lemon thyme rather than rosemary. Do let me know if you try either.

CARROT HALVA

This is a wonderful northern Indian dessert, where the classic combination of saffron, cardamom and rose water works so well with the carrots' sweet, mild earthiness. A carrot cake with these flavours is so good on a wet Sunday afternoon by the fire, or with a cold one in summer, and one day I shall make an ice cream based on this delight. Be aware that this is as sweet as a cherryade shandy, so go easy on the portions.

Serves 4

500g (1lb) carrots, grated
200g (7oz) sugar
350ml (12fl oz) water
pinch of salt
big pinch of saffron, soaked in 2 tbsp water
1 tsp ground cardamom
splash of rose water
100g (3½oz) rice flour
120g (4oz) butter, cubed
2 tbsp pistachios, slivered, finely chopped or blitzed in a food processor
1 tbsp sesame seeds (optional)

Place the grated carrot in a pan with the sugar, water and salt. Bring to the boil, stirring until the sugar has dissolved. Reduce the heat, cover and simmer for 15–20 minutes, stirring occasionally.

Tip into a food processor and purée until smooth and creamy, adding the soaked saffron, cardamom and rose water. Taste and add a little more rose water if you like.

In a large frying pan, toast the rice flour over a low heat, stirring often, for 2–3 minutes until aromatic.

Add the carrot purée to the frying pan, along with the butter, and continue to stir continuously for 5–10 minutes over a low heat until you have a thick and smooth paste.

Spoon the halva into a shallow dish and pack firmly with a spoon. Allow the dish to cool and then garnish with the pistachios. Spoon into dishes, serving it chilled or at room temperature.

Alternatively, once cool, roll the halva into golf-ball-sized globes. Place the pistachios in a shallow dish and combine with the sesame seeds, then roll the halva balls in the mix to coat. If going down this route, it's best to blitz the pistachios to more of a rough powder, but finely chopped will taste just a good.

VEGAN: Use plant-based butter.
GF: Yes.
SEASONAL SWAPS: Squash or sweet potato can be used instead of the carrot.

MELANZANE AL CIOCCOLATO

There is an imaginary me who drives the windy roads of the Amalfi coast in a Lancia Fulvia, visiting numerous lovers each enchanted by my interpretation of this Italian classic. The unimaginary me drives the windy roads of East Devon dad-taxiing my teenage daughter and being assured 'it's really not that bad, and you know how much I hate aubergines'. Take your affirmations wherever they come.

I cannot pretend that this is not sweet, but the gentle bitterness of the chocolate and aubergine – along with the lemon's edge – keep it nicely to attention. Not only is this utterly delicious, it is the simplest of desserts that you can do most of ahead and assemble in moments. The aubergines must be tight as a wedding balloon; peeling a slack aubergine is no one's idea of fun. The lemon should be lively – from Amalfi, if you've really entered into the fantasy.

Serves 4

2 aubergines (eggplants), peeled

olive oil, for frying

100g (3 ½ oz) dark chocolate, broken into pieces

100ml (3 ½ fl oz) coconut milk

60g (2 ¼ oz) pine nuts

60g (2 ¼ oz) caster (superfine) sugar

1 tsp mixed spice

120g (4oz) crème fraîche

120g (4oz) mascarpone

finely grated zest of 1 lemon

2 tbsp tahini

Cut the aubergines lengthways into slices 5–7mm (¼ in) thick. Pour enough oil into a wide frying pan to come 5mm (¼ in) up the sides and warm over a medium-high heat. When hot, carefully lower the aubergine slices into the oil in a single layer – do in batches if needs be. Reduce the heat until the aubergine is frying lightly; the idea is to soften and colour them a little. Turn using tongs and, once cooked, remove to a plate covered with kitchen paper.

In a small pan over a low heat, melt the chocolate into the coconut milk, stirring often, until combined. Remove from the heat.

In a dry frying pan, toast the pine nuts over a medium heat, agitating the pan frequently; you are after a little light colouring rather than full scorch.

Mix the sugar and spice together on a large plate. One slice at a time, dip the aubergine in the spiced sugar to cover all sides.

Stir the crème fraîche, mascarpone and lemon zest together. Smear a little of the mixture on each of four small plates. Arrange half an aubergine's worth of slices on each plate, with a dab more of the lemony mix between each. Drizzle with the tahini, then the chocolate sauce, and sprinkle with the pine nuts. Sit back and dream of the Amalfi coast while you eat it.

VEGAN: Use 240g (8oz) plant-based crème fraîche or whipping cream, or coconut yoghurt, in place of the crème fraîche and mascarpone. It won't have the same richness but will still be enjoyable.
GF: Yes.
SEASONAL SWAPS: With their characteristic bitterness, I suspect fried slices of chicory (endive) and celeriac would work differently well here in place of the aubergine.

BASQUE SWEETCORN CHEESECAKE

I know. You are probably thinking why risk a cheesecake that is perfectly amazing as it is by adding sweetcorn. The answer is because I wouldn't put it in the book if it wasn't at the very least an equally delicious variation and you're going to have to trust me about that. Make it; I promise you'll be delighted. Sweetcorn's bright sweetness sits quietly in the background, present without dominating, and bringing something almost lemony to the flavour. By all means add the finely grated zest of an unwaxed lemon for extra zing if you fancy.

Two things. The sweetcorn can be fresh or canned, but the weight in the recipe is just the kernels. And when lining the buttered tin, make a band twice the height you need it for the side. Snip into it every 7cm (3in) or so to half the height, then line it so that the uncut part of the band is against the side of the tin and the tabs formed by the cuts overlap against the base. This makes the paper sit tightly against the side and a circle placed over the tabs means there are no gaps in the paper lining on the base.

Serves 8

a little butter, for greasing the tin

160g (5½oz) sweetcorn

350g (12oz) crème fraîche

650g (1lb 7oz) cream cheese, softened

220g (7½oz) caster (superfine) sugar

pinch of salt

2 tbsp cornflour (cornstarch)

4 large eggs (at room temperature), whisked

1–2 tbsp icing (confectioner's) sugar (optional)

Preheat the oven to 200°C/180°C fan/400°F and grease and line a 20cm (8in) springform cake tin with baking parchment.

Blend the sweetcorn thoroughly into 100g (3½oz) of the crème fraîche – I find a stick blender in a narrowish cup really good for this.

Whisk the cream cheese in a large bowl until smooth, then add the rest of the crème fraîche, the sweetcorn mixture, sugar, salt and cornflour and whisk again until smooth and thoroughly combined. Add the eggs and whisk until incorporated.

Pour into the prepared tin and tap gently against the work surface to remove any air bubbles. Place in the centre of the oven and bake for about 50 minutes; it should retain the barest wobble.

Cool completely and then chill in the fridge for a couple of hours at least. Release from the tin and dust with icing sugar before serving, if you wish.

VEGAN: No.
GF: Yes.
SEASONAL SWAPS: Lemon and a little cocoa work well in this, but for the most part I'd have sides such as cherries, spiced apple and so on accompanying rather than in the cheesecake itself. That said, an equal weight of the sweet potato purée from page 206 in place of the sweetcorn brings a delicious toffee-ish note, and a little more heft.

SPICED SQUASH + APPLE CAKE

If you like carrot cake, you'll love this: the squash brings a little extra nuttiness, and the apple (along with olive oil in place of the usual butter) keeps everything super moist. You can cut these ingredients to two-thirds for a round cake of 20cm (8in) or so, but this freezes well so I like to make a larger quantity. The cooking time varies with your oven and the exact dimensions of the tin/dish used, so keep an eye on it: check how it's doing after 50 minutes or so. I've made this with the same weight of gluten-free flour and it works a treat, though is perhaps slightly denser, but pleasingly so (so says my GF daughter).

Makes 24

120g (4oz) sultanas (golden raisins)

500g (1lb 2oz) cooking apples, peeled, cored and chopped

2 tbsp ground cardamom

330g (11oz) self-raising flour

1½ tsp baking powder

1 tbsp ground cinnamon

1 tbsp ground ginger

2 tsp ground cloves

1 tsp salt

330g (11oz) soft light brown sugar, plus an extra 5 tbsp for the syrup

180ml (6fl oz) extra virgin olive oil

3 eggs, lightly beaten

finely grated zest and juice of 2 lemons

650g (1lb 7oz) squash, peeled, deseeded and grated, to give around 400g (14oz)

120g (4oz) hazelnuts, roughly chopped

1–2 tbsp icing (confectioner's) sugar (optional)

Soak the sultanas in boiling water for 15 minutes, then drain.

Pour 1cm (½in) water into a medium pan over a medium heat and add the apples and cardamom. Bring to a gentle simmer, stirring occasionally, until it becomes a purée. Allow to cool.

Preheat the oven to 170°C/150°C fan/340°F and line a roughly 20 x 25cm (8 x 10in) baking dish with baking parchment.

Sift the flour into a bowl and mix with the baking powder, spices and salt.

In a large bowl, whisk the sugar and oil until combined, then add the eggs and whisk until creamy. Fold in the apple purée, followed by the spiced flour. Next fold in the lemon zest, grated squash, sultanas and hazelnuts.

Spoon the mixture into the prepared tin and smooth the surface with a spatula. Bake for about 1 hour until a skewer or toothpick inserted comes out without crumbs clinging to it.

Warm the lemon juice and the 5 tablespoons sugar in a small pan over a low heat until the sugar has dissolved, increasing the heat to a simmer for a few minutes to thicken it slightly.

Allow the cake to cool for a few minutes, then pierce the surface with a skewer or similar, pouring the syrup slowly and evenly across it so that it soaks in. Wait at least a few more minutes before cutting and serving, dusted with a little icing sugar.

VEGAN: Try a little silken tofu in place of the eggs, or make it without – the result is denser, more like a brownie.
GF: Yes.
SEASONAL SWAPS: Sweet potato, carrot, celeriac and Jerusalem artichoke all work really well instead of the squash. By all means, try different nuts if you fancy.

MAHENSHA

Like squash, sweet potato's natural sweetness allows you to lean it in different directions by careful choice of spices. More earthy flavours – cumin, coriander and so on – would make this beautifully savoury, or with the spices here, sweet without a hint of cloying. Even with these sweeter spices, a sour drizzle of pomegranate molasses takes them back to ambiguous territory, while a drizzle of honey takes them into full-on sweet.

You can make this as is traditional, as a coiled snake of crisp spiced delight, but these samosa-like triangles invite picking up, with the only quandary being whether one or five is the correct portion.

Makes 12

2 sweet potatoes

100g (3½oz) butter, melted

100g (3½oz) almonds, toasted and finely chopped

100g (3½oz) walnuts, toasted and finely chopped

75g (2½oz) raisins or sultanas

3 tbsp honey

1 tsp ground cinnamon, plus extra for dusting

½ tsp ground ginger

¼ tsp grated nutmeg

¼ tsp ground cloves

1 tsp orange blossom water

8 sheets of filo (phyllo) pastry

2 tbsp icing (confectioner's) sugar

Preheat the oven to 180°C/160°C fan/350°F.

Bake the sweet potatoes until tender. Scoop the soft flesh out into a bowl and mash until smooth. Stir in 25g (1oz) of the butter, and all the almonds, walnuts and raisins. Add the honey, ground spices and orange blossom water, mixing until well combined.

Lay out a sheet of filo and brush with a little of the melted butter; place another sheet on top and brush this with butter too. Cut the filo sheets in thirds down their length. Place a spoonful (about one twelfth of the total) of the filling 6cm (2½in) or so from the end of a pastry strip. Fold the short end of the pastry over the filling to form a triangular shape. Continue folding the pastry strip over the filling; the triangular shape means you wrap each of the three sides alternately. Try to overlap each point a little as this prevents the filling seeping out. Brush the completed parcel with melted butter and place on a baking tray. Repeat the process with the rest of the filo sheets, filling and butter.

Bake for 12–15 minutes until the pastry is golden and crisp. Remove from the oven and let them cool for 15 minutes.

Dust with icing sugar and cinnamon before serving warm or at room temperature.

VEGAN: Use vegan butter.
GF: Use GF filo pastry.
SEASONAL SWAPS: Squash, celeriac, Jerusalem artichokes or carrots work really well in place of the sweet potato.

TOMATO + PLUM CRUMBLE

I had a feeling that the coming together of plums and tomatoes might be as glorious in a crumble as it can be in a late summer salad, and I was right, but it took a few goes. The key step is in cooking the fruit for 10 minutes and draining off the liquid, as otherwise the tomatoes let out so much juice that the crumble won't live up to its name.

Serves 4

300g (10oz) tomatoes, halved or quartered depending on size

500g (1lb 2oz) plums, stoned and sliced

2 tbsp soft light brown sugar

2 tsp lemon thyme leaves

pinch of flaky sea salt

For the crumble

100g (3½oz) rolled oats

50g (2oz) plain (all-purpose) flour

50g (2oz) cold butter, cut into small cubes

50g (2oz) soft light brown sugar

1 tbsp coriander seeds

pinch of flaky sea salt

double (heavy) cream, to serve

Preheat the oven to 200°C/180°C fan/400°F.

In a large bowl, combine the tomatoes, plums, brown sugar, thyme and salt. Transfer to a baking dish about 20 x 15cm (8 x 6in) and bake for 10 minutes to start cooking the fruit, then drain off the excess liquid.

Combine the rolled oats, plain flour, cold cubed butter, brown sugar, coriander seeds and pinch of salt. Use your fingertips to rub the butter in until the mixture resembles coarse crumbs. Sprinkle the crumble topping over the fruit mixture in the baking dish.

Place back in the oven and cook for 25–30 minutes until the topping is golden and the fruit is bubbling and tender. Remove it from the oven and let it rest for 5 minutes before serving with cream.

VEGAN: Use plant-based butter or olive oil, and plant-based cream.
GF: Use GF plain flour and/or GF oats reduced to a flour in a food processor.
SEASONAL SWAPS: This works really well with any stone fruit, such as peaches and nectarines, instead of the plums.

PARSNIP + NUTMEG ICE CREAM

At first taste, this might seem like nutmeg ice cream, with a late wave of sweet parsnip seemingly the magnifier of this marvellous spice, but a few spoonfuls in and what seemed like two voices singing the same note will reveal itself as a duo in perfect harmony. I've had one or two sceptical expressions responding to the offer of this; all have been converted by this joyous creation. As fine a way with parsnips as there is.

Makes about 1.5 litres (2¾ pints)

800ml (1¾ pints) coconut milk
260g (9¼oz) caster (superfine) sugar
600g (1lb 5oz) grated parsnip
5 egg yolks, lightly whisked
⅔ nutmeg, finely grated
pomegranate molasses (optional)

Put the coconut milk and sugar into a large pan and bring to the boil over a medium-high heat, stirring occasionally. Reduce the heat, add the parsnip and egg yolks and simmer, stirring constantly, until the parsnip has cooked and the mixture threatens to coat the back of a spoon. Stir in the nutmeg. Remove from the heat and allow to cool with a tea towel over to prevent a skin forming.

Transfer to a blender and blitz until completely smooth, then churn in an ice-cream maker if you have one and freeze. Alternatively, pour into a plastic tub and freeze for a few hours, whizz in a blender, freeze for another couple of hours, and if you are of conscientious mind and smoothness of texture is critical to you, you can repeat the blending before freezing.

Drizzle with pomegranate molasses when serving, if you fancy.

VEGAN: Instead of the egg yolks, use your fingers to mix 5 teaspoons of cornflour (cornstarch) into a little coconut milk until it forms a smooth paste, and stir in when the milk has reduced to a simmer.
GF: Yes.
SEASONAL SWAPS: Celeriac, sweet potato and Jerusalem artichokes make differently delightful versions.

CUCUMBER MOJITO GRANITA

It's all but impossible not to like a mojito, and this takes its spirit – a cool sea breeze, when the sun is high – and changes its state to solid. Bright, sweet-sharp, aromatic, refreshing and with a little rum nudge, it just tastes cold, like schoolyard Extra Strong Mints. If you want to churn this into a smooth sorbet in an ice-cream maker by all means do; an aversion to washing up, and the pleasure in the coarser texture of a granita mean I rarely do.

Makes about 600ml (1¼ pints), depending on the size and juiciness of your cucumber

200g (7oz) caster (superfine) sugar

generous bunch of mint, leaves only

1kg (2lb 4oz) cucumber, peeled and deseeded

45ml (3 tbsp) white rum

juice of 2 limes

Stir the sugar into 150ml (5fl oz) just-boiled water until dissolved. Add the mint leaves and allow to infuse until completely cool. Remove and discard the mint.

Blitz the cucumber in a high-speed blender until entirely liquid.

Stir the mint syrup, the rum and lime juice into the cucumber juice. Pour into a freezer-friendly container and freeze.

To serve, use a fork to scratch up crystals of refreshment into a small glass.

VEGAN: Yes.
GF: Yes.
SEASONAL SWAPS: I wouldn't try this with parsnips…

INDEX

THANK YOU

I am extremely lucky to work with a special team. To Harriet Webster (harrietwebster.com), equal parts project manager, incisive editor, stylist, wise words, keen ear and great fun; to Matt Cox of Newman and Eastwood (newmanandeastwood.com), a brilliant designer of such taste and creativity; to Claire Rochford (clairerochford.co.uk) for excellent creative direction and support; to Matt Williamson for being the most extraordinary shoot chef, collaborator, and possessor of the most insulting mouth; to Clare Sayer, once again, for your incisive and sensitive copy editing: I am embarrassed (but glad) to include your names not on the cover where they belong, but at the back of this book. Thank you so much for being such a part of making this book what it is.

To Sarah Lavelle, thank you for having me as part of your Quadrille family and your caring stewardship of such a great list. Thank you also to Becky Smedley, Laura Willis and Laura Eldridge at Quadrille for your lively marketing and publicity.

A huge thank you to Laura Creyke at Mark Hutchinson Management for your energetic, creative PR and excellent company.

As ever, a huge thank you to Caroline Michel at PFD, for your support, enthusiasm and guidance.

Thanks to Cris Barnett (cristianbarnett.com) – brilliant photographer and excellent man – for the portraits, and to The Pig at Combe (thepighotel.com/at-combe) for allowing us to use their wonderful garden for the shoot. And lastly, to Netherton Foundry (netherton-foundry. co.uk) who make the best pans, and I say that with pleasure rather than payment.

And thank you to those greatly admired writers who have been kind enough to say such generous words about this book: it is much appreciated.

Thank you all for making it such a pleasure to do what I most enjoy doing.

ABOUT THE AUTHOR

Mark Diacono is lucky enough to spend most of his time eating, growing, writing and talking about food. He has written a number of award-winning books, including *A Year at Otter Farm* and *A Taste of the Unexpected* (which both won Food Book of the Year for André Simon and the Guild of Food Writers, respectively), *Sour* (which was Food Book of the Year 2019 in *The Sunday Times* and *Daily Mail*, and nominated for a James Beard Award in the US), *Herb* and *Spice*.

Known for growing everything from Szechuan pepper to pecans to Asian pears, Mark's refreshing approach to growing and eating has done much to inspire a new generation to grow some of what they eat. He was involved with River Cottage, appearing in the TV series, running courses and events at River Cottage HQ, and he has written four River Cottage books. Mark also writes regularly for a range of publications including *The Telegraph*, *Delicious* and *Country Life*, and his features have appeared in *The Observer*, *Guardian*, *National Geographic*, and others. He also speaks and demos at food festivals around the UK and writes for an engaged and growing audience on his Substack: 'Mark Diacono's Imperfect Umbrella'.

Cook's notes
All recipes serve 4, unless otherwise stated
Eggs are medium, and free-range, unless otherwise stated
Parsley is always flat-leaf
Sea salt is used throughout
Extra virgin olive oil is used throughout

In some places I have suggested cheeses that are not traditionally vegetarian, namely Parmesan, feta, taleggio and Gruyère. If needed, please do seek out their now commonly available vegetarian counterparts, or plant-based alternatives.

Although plant-based substitutes are better than ever, different brands/types do vary, so please play around with some of the recipes and see what works best for you.

Managing Director Sarah Lavelle
Commissioning & Project Editor Harriet Webster
Copy Editor Clare Sayer
Designer Matt Cox at Newman+Eastwood
Photographer Mark Diacono
Food Stylist Matt Williamson
Head of Production Stephen Lang
Senior Production Controller Sabeena Atchia

First published in 2024 by Quadrille, an imprint of Hardie Grant Publishing

Quadrille
52–54 Southwark Street
London SE1 1UN
quadrille.com

ISBN: 978 1 83783 054 1
Printed in China

MIX
Paper | Supporting
responsible forestry
FSC
www.fsc.org   FSC™ C020056